NEW MEN for NEW TIMES

NEW MEN
for NEW TIMES

A Christian Philosophy of Education

by Beatrice Avalos

SHEED AND WARD · NEW YORK

ACKNOWLEDGMENT

The quotations from the New Testament in this book are taken from *The New Testament in English,* translated by Ronald Knox.

CONTENTS

1   EDUCATION IN THE CONTEXT OF TIME   3

2   MAN AND SOCIETY IN THE PERSPECTIVES
    OF NATURALISM   29

3   MAN IN A CHRISTIAN PERSPECTIVE   79

4   EDUCATING THE "NEW MAN" FOR THE
    "NEW COMMUNITY"   120

NEW MEN for NEW TIMES

1

EDUCATION
IN THE CONTEXT OF TIME

EVERY EDUCATIONAL THEORY enshrines some notion of human perfection which serves as a lodestar to developments in the practical sphere. Tonalities in form certainly differ, but as we examine the history of educational thought from Plato to Dewey we find throughout a common aim: to provide insight into the ways and means by which man can be helped to reach fulfillment as a human being.

In Christian educational thought this common goal of human perfection reaches back to the ideal set by Christ before all mankind: ". . . you are to be perfect, as your heavenly Father is perfect" (Matt. 5:48). It has since then become the task of Christian thought to arrive at an understanding of what this perfection means, and of Christian educational thought to apply this understanding to the determination of educational principles and practices.

An ideal of human perfection, and hence a conception of the nature of man and of his existential reality, belongs to the very essence of educational theory; and as a corollary, we may say that the practical effectiveness of education will depend on the validity of our specific mode of understanding man.

In the Thomistic tradition there is an axiom which expresses the nature of the links between the being or mode of being of a thing and its activities: *operari sequitur esse et modum operandi modum essendi*. This principle implies that all activities of a practical nature, primarily those with ethical and educational connotations, are definitely related to and flow from the being and mode of being of its subject, that is, of man.

If we now consider the mode of being of man we find that he not only exists in himself and for himself (a substantial reality) but that he also exists in a wider reality to which he is related and which is related to him. Man is connected with the rest of nature and with his fellow-men through his bodily form and needs and through the activities which distinguish him as a human being, namely, knowledge and love. He is also, because of his position in the hierarchy of being, in a relation to that form of reality which transcends natural experience, the supernatural order. Through grace the totality of his being and activities may be oriented in a new way. In all of these relations man is at the same time inserted in a given temporal moment, a moment which determines new modalities in his way of existing as a being-in-relation.

It is this reality of man in himself and of man in his relations that St. Thomas visualized as an ordered reality in which every degree of being and operations is hierarchically related to each other in view of the Perfect Being.[1] Our knowledge of man rests upon our understanding of this whole order of reality, and so also, in a more specific way, does our understanding of the nature of educational activities. This consideration of man as a reality in himself and as related to a wider reality leads us to state as the fundamental presupposition, which will guide our reflections in this work, a slight

[1] Cf. *De Pot. Dei,* 7.9; *Contra Gentiles,* 3.90.

modification of the *operari sequitur esse* principle. We will consider that in education it is always the entire order of reality or being that must determine the order of its activities: *ordo essendi est ordo agendi.*

The above principle demands that we study what God tells us of man in his relation to reality (with the aid of theology) and what we ourselves learn about man in his relations through reflection upon human activities and upon the temporal framework which nurtures him (with the aid of philosophy and the empirical disciplines such as psychology and sociology). We must realize that a consideration of the *ordo essendi* as the guiding principle for educational activities does not imply adherence to a pattern of static formulae. If the history of educational thought has revealed the concern of generation after generation with the problem of education, we can surmise that educational principles can not be inflexibly applied in *all* epochs in the same way, precisely because the *ordo essendi* is never once and for all known. Although in philosophy we may speak of a *philosophia perennis,* and although the content of revelation was completed with the death of the last apostle, there is still room for an examination of our Christian heritage and the formulation of new principles (in the light of philosophy and theology) which conform to the new situations that present themselves as history moves on.

It is in the light of the above reflections that we must acknowledge a double dimension in the order of being, or *ordo essendi*: a *fixed* or permanent aspect, and a *dynamic* or adaptable one. In its fixed dimension the *ordo essendi,* as manifest through revelation, points to the first lines of Genesis: "Let us make man in our image and likeness" (1:26). This is forever the real status of man—an image and likeness of God. It makes no difference to the nature of his being whether man rejects or unites himself to God—he still retains his resemblance to the divine nature; his soul remains spiritual. Philosophically we may speak in terms of Aristotelian-Thomistic thought and say that man is a contingent being who partakes of an animal and a spiritual nature, who is marked as human by those operations which derive from his spiritual nature, knowledge and love, along with the possibility of self-determination and self-realization granted by human liberty.

In the fixed dimension of the *ordo essendi* we thus see man as a being created by God and destined for Him, a relation which remains metaphysically indestructible. We further see man as himself related to every other creature in the whole order of the universe through his activities, and, in a special way, through his powers of knowing and loving. However, there is also a dynamism which we observe in our experiential contact with reality. We see changes in nature, we are aware of changes in man from infancy through adulthood, and we observe changes in the cultural situation which in turn affect man. These are all changes which point to the metaphysical structure of being, to the way traversed from potency to act that characterizes every contingent being. We are aware of the dynamic qualities in man not only through experiential evidence and our metaphysical insight into the nature of being, but also through the revealed truths of the Fall and the Redemption. We are conscious at the same time of human imperfection and of perfection as a goal—all of which suggests a *way* toward perfection. Hence we assert not only that man is created in God's image and likeness but that he must incessantly strive to realize this image more fully. Not only is man redeemed by Christ, he must also endeavor to make himself *like* Christ. It belongs to the very nature of man's distinctive activities that they perfect him. The regulating or exemplary cause of this process consists ultimately in the realization of the image of God through the development of human nature toward a perfection modeled after Christ, in whom human and divine nature find a fulfilled unity.

These are the elements which give to the *ordo essendi* its dynamic connotations. Applied to man we must say that the understanding of his way to perfection at a given moment depends upon an understanding of the conditions in the order of reality to which he is related at that same moment, or, better still, an understanding of what we may call the existential condition of man.

If we consider for a moment the Christian view of history which sees the providential guidance of God in temporal events and the development of His divine plan through them, we are able to view the particular temporal conditions of a period as the natural setting for the realization of human perfection, and we can conclude that every historical epoch will realize in a different modality the common ideal of human perfection.

The above considerations lead us again to reflect upon the nature of educational theory. If educational activities as such are to be guided by the axiom *ordo essendi est ordo agendi,* and if we do not conceive of the *ordo essendi* only in its fixed dimensions, then we must acknowledge that educational theory and, consequently, practice must take account of the dynamic dimensions of the order of reality and man as given in a particular time. To understand the *ordo essendi* we must then consider the characteristics and conditions of the times. Every man must become, in the last analysis, a "child of his times," not in the sense of yielding to and being absorbed by the times, but in the sense of knowing them, appreciating their values and recognizing their dangers so as to master them in the pursuit of his ultimate end.

To be a full human being he [man] must indeed become a citizen of the universe, simply man, but to be a fully formed human individual he must find his individualized growth within his own time and his own culture; he must live in his own age and in his own time, knowing its distinctive realization of human living and assuming its distinctive forms of responsibility.[2]

In the light of this, educational thought, and particularly Catholic educational thought inasmuch as it is deeply committed to the highest ideal of human perfection, must consider the conditions of the man of our century and thus contribute toward a time-conditioned meaning of the perennial ideal of perfection expressed in Christ's call to be like the Father. And as a consequence, there should be a revitalization of the statements and principles which guide educational practices.

MAN IN THE CONTEMPORARY WORLD

Ever since the early part of our century there has been a growing awareness of a unique turning-point in history,[3] the result, for the most part, of the developments which broke upon the world in the fifteenth, sixteenth, and seventeenth centuries. The widening of the horizons of the known world by exploration; the development of the physico-mathematical

[2] This statement was part of a general definition of the role of the Catholic Liberal Arts college in its task of turning out men able to cope with the situation of contemporary American society, particularly in the intellectual field. Robert J. Henle (Dean of the Graduate School, St. Louis University), "Objectives of the Catholic Liberal Arts College," 7. (Mimeographed.)

[3] See, for example, Oswald Spengler's *The Decline of the West* and José Ortega y Gasset, *The Revolution of the Masses,* both written in the earlier part of the century in response to a situation which they found equivalent to the disturbed period following the decline of classical culture and the breakdown of the Roman Empire.

sciences and their application to the most varied fields of human endeavor, notably technology; the emergence of religious pluralism in once unified Christendom; and the revolution in thought brought about by Descartes' break with philosophical tradition which culminated in religious nihilism or atheism—all of these factors, alone and in interaction, had transformed the cultural situation in the Western world before the beginning, in the nineteenth century, of a new era imbued with the Darwinian concept of the universe. Today we look at our century as one of amazingly rapid changes and incredible discoveries. Empirical science has provided us with the means necessary for the conquest of space and at the same time with the weapons capable of destroying humanity. The functionalization of work, the mechanization of life, the urbanization of vast areas and the growth of the "organization" have enormously complicated the social structure. Political unrest marks the situation of many lands which are awakening to the new cultural conditions and wish to assert themselves in these conditions. Revolutionary discoveries in psychology and sociology have laid open elements in human nature unknown or ignored until now. And in the midst of this century of change, the intellectual elite feels the challenge of applying the Darwinian explanation of nature to an evolutionary interpretation of reality conceived only as a reality-in-nature.

A time of changes such as ours has also posed the conditions for crisis. The great events of the century, in particular the two world wars with their immediate effects and after-effects, have given content to and expressed the gravity of the contemporary situation, thus impressing upon historians, sociologists, and social philosophers the realization that we are today facing a real crisis.

It has been this convulsed state of our world that has offered a starting-point to the meditative analysis of the situation of man which characterizes the existentialist group of philosophers. Because their critique reflects to a great extent the descriptions of the contemporary world offered by a number of different sources, and because it seeks to penetrate beyond the level of description to ponder the deeper causes of, and the implications contained in, the modern condition, it seems to us profitable to utilize their approach in our effort to understand the man of our times.

The existentialist movement finds its roots in the nineteenth century in two important thinkers, Kierkegaard and Nietzsche, who almost prophetically described to us not only the man of their times but also the man of the future, a potential product of the conditions of their epoch.

After a century of individualism, the developments of empirical science and technology which brought men externally closer while mechanizing their activities, and the intellectual trend toward a monistic view of reality, especially human reality—such as Hegel's—had their combined effects upon the nineteenth century, opening the way for an era of the masses, of collectivism. Reflecting on this situation, existentialists from Kierkegaard to Marcel have all, with different emphases, concentrated their attention on the position of man in a society whose forces and elements seem more and more to suppress the existence of the individual in his personal or unique reality—to produce the type of man who does not distinguish himself from the group but surrenders his uniqueness to it.

Dividing between them the span of the nineteenth century, Kierkegaard and Nietzsche agreed in pointing to the growth of a conformist attitude, an attitude which in Nietzsche's opinion was undermining the "wholeness" of European culture. Kierkegaard spoke of the "crowd" mentality which discour-

aged all individual opinions and efforts. Nowhere could he
find ten men afraid of harboring a wrong opinion, but he was
able to find thousands afraid of standing alone even with a
right opinion, and ready to acquiesce in "public opinion" as
proclaimed by the press. The so-called Christian life led by
the members of the Danish Established Church was another
example of that conformism, the mass or bourgeois mentality,
which Kierkegaard had detected in the wider circles of society.
He accused Christians of yielding to a "comfortable" Christianity while forgetting the way of the cross to eternal blessed-
ness. He challenged the conviction that everybody should be
Christian just because of being born in a Christian state. Such
an understanding of the Christian life could only contribute
to a mediocre and watered-down Christianity.

For Nietzsche the bourgeois conformist mentality described
by Kierkegaard was simply "nihilism," that is, the repudiation
of all that is of worth, value and dignity in the individual. In
his *Thoughts Out of Season,* Nietzsche leveled an impassioned
attack against the German culture in his day, an indictment
implicitly directed against the whole of European culture. His
complaint was that education, and in particular the way in
which acquaintance with the historical tradition of the culture
was being made—through a rapid inculcation of facts—was
undermining the depth of comprehension and intellectual de-
tachment which true contact with great historical figures
should afford. In lieu of a strong, energetic personality, he
asserted, we have a man who is "turned into a restless, dilet-
tante spectator, and arrives at a condition when even great
wars and revolutions cannot affect him beyond the moment."[4]
Conformity was for Nietzsche the distinguishing trait of the

[4] F. W. Nietzsche, "The Use and Abuse of History," *Thoughts
Out of Season,* trans. Adrian Collins (Edinburgh: T. N. Foulis, 1909),
Part II, p. 39.

age, a product of the tendency toward "equalization." He believed that man is aware of his uniqueness but surrenders it "from fear of his neighbour, who looks for the latest conventionalities in him, and is wrapped up in them himself."[5]

In Nietzsche's opinion the developments of the age were largely to blame for this situation of man, and he strongly emphasized the destructive effects of the machine on human personality, the evils of the press in its making of "public opinion," which he saw as the only medium through which the man of his time, increasingly incapable of independent reflection, could feel any security. In prophetic tones he asserted that "the press, the machine, the railway, the telegraph are premises from which no one has yet dared to draw the conclusions that will follow in a thousand years."[6]

As the concomitant of the individual's surrender to a "crowd" mentality, Kierkegaard saw also that, paradoxically, man was alone. As a unit in a great abstract totality, man "no longer belonged to God, to himself, to his beloved, to his art or to his science"[7]; he was in truth, while believing himself to be fully in the world, a displaced man.

Both Kierkegaard and Nietzsche in their analysis of the situation of man sought for the underlying causes, in the light of which they attempted to provide guidelines for a solution. For Kierkegaard it was plain that two factors in particular were responsible: one was the growing development of technology and of industry, with their effects upon the economy and the structure of social life, especially in the cities; the

[5] Nietzsche, "Schopenhauer as an Educator," *Thoughts Out of Season,* Part II, p. 103.

[6] Nietzsche, *Human All-Too-Human,* trans. Helen Zimmern (Edinburgh: T. N. Foulis, 1910), Part II, p. 332.

[7] Søren Kierkegaard, *The Present Age,* trans. Alexander Dru and Walter Lowrie (London: Oxford University Press, 1949), p. 29.

other was the adherence to the Hegelian interpretation of reality. After receiving an education in the Hegelian tradition, Kierkegaard had convinced himself that Hegel's concept of the Idea and the dialectical process simply reduced the individual human person to a moment in the self-unfolding of the Idea. This in turn, he contended, led to the substitution of speculation about the Idea for personal moral responsibility and for a personal relation to God. Men already weakened by the conditions of society, and plunged deeper into their weakness by an ideology which denied their individual reality, were unable to fulfill in their lives the three spheres of authentic individual existence. Man in the spontaneous life of his senses, in the exercise of reason as an end in itself—the *aesthetic* sphere of human life—is empty if not possessed of the sense of responsibility, expressed in the assertion of the will, that the second sphere, the sphere of *ethical* life, confers. And without the crowning of human life through a personal relation to God—the *religious* sphere—man is a mutilated being. But this last sphere is one dependent upon faith, and faith essentially involves a leap into transcendence requiring the exercise of human liberty, and hence not subject to mass techniques. Consequently the mass man of his time was lacking in humanity because unable to crown his existence with a free act of faith and, consequently again, for a full human existence the solution could only lie in the reassertion of the individual's personal reality. Hence we have Kierkegaard's almost one-sided stress on the individual at the expense of the community. And for Kierkegaard the individual—that is, the true man—is he who is possessed of one great idea in the light of which he decides everything, according to which he molds his life, and for which he is prepared to live and die.

In Nietzsche's opinion the situation of man as he witnessed

it was the result of a cleavage between the state of belief in
the men of the century and the nominally accepted set of
norms for their lives. In the Middle Ages when faith was
strong there had been a consciousness of sin because belief in
God guaranteed the validity of the moral code to which men
adhered. Since then, as Nietzsche saw it, God had been
eradicated; nevertheless men continued to hold to a morality
with no meaning in itself—one which, on this account, forced
them into an equalized, a "herd" way of life. This adherence
to Christian morality was, in the last analysis, the cause of the
mass man. And like Kierkegaard, Nietzsche asserted that only
one solution could save man—namely, to place emphasis on
a re-evaluation of the dignity and worth of the individual. But
this was to be done—on the basic premise of God's death—
by means of an entirely new and this-worldly set of values
and norms, a code which would elevate a select few to the
heights of the "superman," thus saving in those few the flower
of humanity.

It was Nietzsche's achievement to show how atheism leads
to nihilism, to the phenomenon of the "culture-philistine" he
so wholeheartedly despised; to show how nihilism in turn is
productive of a moral vacuum in which man plunges to a
depth below the level of animal life. It was also Nietzsche's
genius to perceive that once man reaches that condition something must be done to re-establish him in his individual human
existence. The question that remains open, however, is whether
it is necessary to postulate the death of God in order to restore
the lost human dignity.

Turning to our century, we find Karl Jaspers and Gabriel
Marcel observing, like many others among their fellow-exis-
tentialists, that these nineteenth-century developments are now

producing the fruits which Nietzsche and Kierkegaard already saw in germ in their contemporaries.

Jaspers is aware that in the midst of a time of change and of true crisis[8] the need to understand the situation of man and to effect a reappraisal of his nature in terms of his actual condition is imperative. His critique of *Dasein* (the "unauthentic" existence of man in his present condition) and his concern for *Existenz* (what "authentic" human existence should be) are an index of this conviction, which is shared by Marcel.[9]

Both Jaspers and Marcel acknowledge the existence of a functionalized mass man, the slave of the mechanisms of society and of the conditions which govern his life in society. Marcel asserts that all things within man and outside of him "conspire to identify this man with his functions—meaning not only his functions as worker, as trade union member or as voter, but with his vital functions as well."[10] Such a functionalization, as Jaspers in turn sees it, deprives man of that which constitutes him as an independent human being:

Nothing appeals to him with the verity of substantial being. Whether in enjoyment or discomfort, whether strenuous or fatigued, he is still nothing more than the function of his daily task. As he lives on from day to day, the only desire that may stir him

[8] In his most recent books, especially *Die Atombombe und die Zukunft des Menschen* (Muenchen: R. Piper & Co. Verlag, 1958), Jaspers has declared that we must acknowledge the real critical elements contained in the possibility of the destruction of human civilization through atomic warfare. He asserts that "the history of mankind no longer has only spiritual crises to contend with but that it also faces real crises which will result in either the decay of humanity or a new reality of humanness itself." *Op. cit.*, p. 252.

[9] Marcel's opposition is between *having* (sphere of "unauthentic" existence, and *being* (sphere of "authentic" existence).

[10] Marcel, *The Philosophy of Existence*, trans. Manya Harari (New York: Philosophical Library, 1949), p. 2.

beyond that of performing this task is the desire to occupy the best obtainable place in the apparatus.[11]

"Techniques of degradation," as Marcel calls some of the products of modern technology, such as the mass media of communication, are responsible for a destruction of the sense of personal value in man. Through them, men lose the awareness of themselves and are vulnerable to those powers which seek to reduce them to an atom within a totality. Once the individual is deprived, both in his consciousness and in his concrete existence, of that substantial reality which was linked to his individuality or to the fact of belonging to a small group, it is possible to compel this individual's adherence to what he calls an "abstraction," i.e. an entity (the "State" or the "Party") arising at the impulse of some passion and not from a consideration of objective reality. In this way, Marcel explains the acceptance of totalitarian regimes and the brutalization of the individual in his attitude toward those who have been singled out for him as an "it" which must be destroyed: the "communist" or the "Jew."

The functionalization of the individual is an index of the situation of community life. Jaspers asserts that with the loss of personal selfhood, the community loses one of the essential elements of organized life: proper leadership. Under the rule of the mass, "great" men move to the background while the "efficient" (in fitting into the mechanism) step forward. With the loss of the "person" in man, the sense of responsibility and the understanding which must necessarily guide community life disappear.

A society composed of mass, functionalized units brings about a crisis of values and reinforces the degraded condition

[11] Jaspers, *Man in the Modern Age,* trans. Eden and Cedar Paul (Garden City, New York: Doubleday & Co., 1957), p. 51.

of man. Marcel explains that in the type of thinking manifested by the "crowd," such words as "virtue" and "happiness" lose their meaning because of the fresh modalities they assume with each change of mood.

"Uprootedness" is the word which best describes the situation of man as visualized by the existentialists, and particularly by Jaspers. A time like ours, of constant change in the economic, social, and political situation, of continuous discoveries offering to man both superb possibilities and grave dangers, has contributed to loosening the ties that hitherto gave man a sense of security. Social mobility, due to the unity of the globe and the perfection of the means of communication, has uprooted the individual from his earlier firm attachment to a place, particularly a home. Jaspers asserts that the herding of masses together in big apartment buildings which resemble barracks, the transformation of the home into a mere sleeping place, and the ever increasing technicization of daily life tend to make people indifferent to an environment which they can easily change and to which they do not attach themselves by strong spiritual ties. The ties that formerly bound an individual to his work and the products of his work are disappearing more and more as the splitting and mechanization of activities increases. It is this situation which makes man another replaceable gadget in the great laboring machine and takes away that creativity which sustains the joy he needs to find in his work.

By fitting in and adapting himself to the mechanisms of social life man sacrifices the element of security which a personal awareness of responsible selfhood entails and which is reinforced by a set of spiritualized bonds with reality. In the mass, man no longer is his isolated self, but becomes "an isolated atom whose individual craving to exist has been sacrificed, since the fiction of general equality prevails."[12] Life in our impersonal modern society would thus be consonant with a radical individual aloneness.

The uprootedness of the individual is expressed also in the dissolution of religious bonds—above all, in a Sunday but not workday religion. Jaspers, like Nietzsche, speaks of the "nihilistic" attitude of our generation which has confined religion to a domain unconnected with the rest of life.

The insecurity and loneliness which a dissolution of personal bonds with his fellow-men, with his home, with work, produces in the individual, made more acute by the lack of religious faith, push him to other sources of security—particularly to what Jaspers calls a "blind faith":

Such a faith is an immense substitute, is fragile and suddenly discarded again; it may embrace the most singular contents; it may be, as it were, an empty faith of mere motion. It interprets itself as a feeling of oneness with nature, with world history. It takes concrete shapes in programmes of salvation. It encloses itself in pseudo-scientific total conceptions, in Marxism, in psychoanalysis, in the theory of the race (whose scientific elements, which seldom emerge with clarity, are at the same time beyond doubt).[13]

The foregoing reflections lead Jaspers to the conclusion that there is an evident need to direct our efforts toward a new emphasis on the selfhood of man but without disjoining this understanding from that of man in his relations—above all, his relations to his fellow-men (so important in a mass society) and to a Transcendent (God).

One must consider that the self is always in a situation, placed in the world and in the midst of specific historical

[12] Jaspers, *Man in the Modern Age*, p. 39.
[13] Jaspers, *The Origin and Goal of History*, trans. Michael Bullock (London: Routledge & Kegan Paul Ltd., 1953), p. 132.

circumstances. In this condition man must make decisions—
he must take a position in face of his world, conscious of the
involvement in his situation but also in fidelity to the supra-
spatial and supra-temporal values of his self. The precious
tool here is *liberty*—and it is this tool which is discarded by
the mass man and society. There are risks and limit-situations
which condition the use of liberty, but they are precisely what
gives meaning to human liberty. Liberty, in its deepest meaning, is an invitation to transcendence. First of all, a transcendence in relation to others on the basis of communication. Such
a transcendence is the foundation of the authentic spiritual
community which must come to give soul to the contemporary
mechanized society. This type of community is based on the
mutual knowledge and mutual help of two individual existents.
Communication excludes all that is objective and material;
it is free, gratuitous, total. It implies, on the part of the
individuals involved, first *solitude* and then a *free* movement
of union. It is an immediate contact of two existences, and
its most profound source is *love*. Secondly, there is a transcendence toward what Jaspers calls the Transcendent (his
notion of God). Such a transcendence is aided by attention
to such "clues" as are present in the world and its events, and
it is a transcendence without which the selfhood of man is
only incompletely attained.

That there has been a breakdown in real communication is
also the conclusion arrived at by Marcel from examining man's
condition at its roots. He speaks of a fading away of "intersubjectivity," or the possibility of human communication. This
is so because relations between individuals are those between
a *who* and a *what*, an external relation based on things held
in common (the sphere of having) which does not touch the
central self of the ones relating. The only way to live humanly

in society is by means of relations which involve an *I* and a *Thou*, relations which emerge in each case from the center of the personality, from what each *is* (sphere of being). It also requires man to become aware, through an act of reflection and moral judgment, of the factual circumstances of his life and situation in the world. Unless he has a clear image of the situation of man everywhere around him and of his participation in this situation, his self-image will be degraded. The consequence of this is simple: "Man depends, to a very great degree, on the idea he has of himself and . . . this idea cannot be degraded without at the same time degrading man."[14]

Like Jaspers, Marcel asserts that a subtle manipulation through propaganda and "degrading techniques" robs man of the use of his freedom, the instrument he has for self-realization. To save freedom, there must be an appeal to intersubjectivity and to a personal communication with God—in other words, the appeal to transcendence of which Jaspers speaks. Self-realization is a work of freedom, and freedom is truly exercised only through an open attitude toward others, an attitude which essentially rests upon love and truth. Above all love—but love in Marcel's view receives its meaning only through its reference to the doctrine of the Mystical Body and through the consequent permeation of human life by grace. Freedom in its truest meaning is found in the service of grace. The possibility of communication among real persons ultimately rests on the link between God and man. In our world "human beings can be linked to each other by a real bond only because, in another dimension, they are linked to something which transcends them and comprehends them in itself."[15] And

[14] Marcel, *Man Against Mass Society*, trans. G. S. Fraser (Chicago: Henry Regnery Company, 1952), p. 14.
[15] *Ibid.*, p. 194.

Marcel concludes that a man who is detached from God in a world like the contemporary one will, as in Sartre's existentialism, strive to assert his selfhood by a sort of auto-divinization while at the same time, and for the same reasons, feeling like a kind of waste product in a meaningless universe.

CONTEMPORARY MAN POSES A CHALLENGE

A short characterization of the situation criticized by the existentialists we have been dealing with would be that of a "mass" society composed of "depersonalized" men, unaware of and failing to exhibit their distinctive human traits. The "depersonalized" man is one who, so far as the observer can see, finds his being outside himself, in the whirlpool of the "others." He feels, he thinks, and he acts like those in whom he sees an embodiment of the current trends in his group and in society. He is the slave of fads, of transient opinions. He reads very little, and in most cases only "best sellers" or material which appeals to his senses and imagination. He watches image after image disappear on his television set without leaving a durable impression on him or arousing critical thought. In a word, this man is externally a "conformist," a man of "bourgeois mentality," of short-sighted and mediocre goals, who wants to enjoy the present with the means offered by the present. Unaware of the uniqueness of his own mode of being, he allows himself to be increasingly engulfed in the stream of society and the multiplicity of its enormous organizations until his face fades away and is fused with all the other faces into one formless structure: the mass.

But this situation is not just the product of the force of attraction of "majority" trends in society; it has a deeper source in the internal condition of a man who has been subject (and with a more intense pressure in the nineteenth and twentieth centuries) to a social, economic and political situation constantly growing in complexity, searching to find himself within it and yet unable to do so. The uprootedness described by Jaspers is simply an effect in the social sphere of the dissolution of the bonds which formerly gave man the security needed to know himself, believe in himself, and assert himself as a unique person. Supported by a community of interests and values (a world of personal relations sustained by the bond of love), rooted in a home symbolic of such a community, attached to nature, and secured by strong religious ties in all his beliefs and relations, man could retain a sense of independence and personal identity in face of the forces of society. But with these elements of security gone, man as a dependent and contingent being surrenders his personal reality for a new security rooted in the mass organization. And this describes the depersonalized man whom existentialists see to a great extent in contemporary man, and of whose existence they hope to make us aware. They are not the only group that is trying to do this. From different points of view we confront this image of man in modern literature and art and in the reflections of sociologists, social pyschologists and social philosophers.[16]

[16] In his article on "The Loneliness of Man," Thurston N. Davis presents some evidence on this point from art and literature. Referring to an exhibition in the New York Museum of Modern Art, he quotes Norris Clarke as saying that "almost every artist lays him [modern man] bare in his own arresting way, as a creature of taut, often agonizing tension, confused as to who and what he is, painfully lonely and isolated from his brothers, the depersonalized victim of his own triumphant technology or of dark primitive forces unleashed from his own subhuman depths." He makes reference also to Archibald MacLeish's *J.B.*, a symbol of the alienated and tortured man living without the security of grace in a world of cataclysmic personal tragedies. *America* (February 6, 1960), 550.

These reflections, coupled with those from our own experience, should persuade us of the existence of a situation which

---

In an analysis of philosophy and philosophers in the modern world, Albert W. Levi centers their thought around two problems, one of which is posed in an excellent introductory chapter to his book. He depicts it as a condition of multiplicity and division of the person, society and human thought. At the personal level it is rootlessness and a loss of security that marks man. The avant-garde literature of Joyce, Pound, and Gertrude Stein is an expression of their lives as expatriates. Levi asserts: "rootless, they mirrored the rootlessness of an age and where they expressed hope it was for their craft and not for an integrated society. The growth of modern science and the heavy industrialization consequent upon it have removed from society the sense of totality and unified effort, dispersing the knowledge of the mechanisms of society into all directions of the wind, making them incomprehensible to man, and spiritually isolating him from his fellows. The lack of a general consensus of belief guaranteed by an intellectual elite has finally led to a disintegrated intellectual plurality which in turn affects the individual's personal situation." Albert William Levi, *Philosophy and the Modern World* (Bloomington: Indiana University Press, 1959).

The voice of sociologists is added to this clamor. Hendrick de Man, a Dutch thinker with socialist leanings, has written an excellent study on the traits of the mass culture, and in it he has pointed to the lonely insecure condition of man in the face of the anonymous forces which impel the mechanism of society and whose aims he cannot see or comprehend. He points to the contributing effects of a devaluation of standards and a consequent lack of direction in human life. Cf. *Vermassung und Kulturverfall* (Muenchen: Leo Lehnen Verlag, 1952).

In his works, Erich Fromm has underlined the problem of conformity in modern society and the inability of man to use his reason, to make decisions; the erroneous understanding of freedom and the consequent danger of submission to authoritarian figures, the potential rulers of totalitarian regimes. He has studied the psychological conditions of the insecure man, incapable of loving, and suffering from a defect of spontaneity and individuality. Cf. especially: *Escape from Freedom, the Sane Society, The Art of Loving.*

Faced with the threat to human civilization that new mortal weapons present, man is prone to what Arnold Toynbee speaks of as "conditioning." He asserts that it is a situation in which the individual surrenders permanently his capacity to think and to will, and his responsibility for moral integrity. Man has a choice today: to descend

is real not only in Europe, for the most part the scene of the
existentialists' observations, but also in America.[17]

To understand the problem the thinkers with whom we
have dealt (especially Jaspers and Marcel) are pointing to, it
is well to bear in mind two of their main emphases: first of all,
on the need for awareness; and secondly on the need to work
for a reassertion of man in his personal reality and for a

the cliff of time to the ledge of inhumanity by yielding to the "ant"
existence brought about by "conditioning." He can also climb to the
next invisible ledge, and this will entail a personal preservation of
freedom and responsibility by a struggle against the forces of conditioning. Cf. Arnold J. Toynbee, *A Study of History*, Vol. XII, *Reconsiderations* (London: Oxford University Press, 1961), pp. 563–565.

Pius XII, in his Christmas Message of 1944, pointed out as one of
the sources of the war devastation he was witnessing, the problem of
the masses. If a new era of peace is to be achieved, he asserted, then
the masses must be replaced by a genuine "people." The Pope's
characterization of the masses merits comparison with contemporary
man: "the masses are inert of themselves and can only be moved from
outside"; they are "an easy plaything in the hands of anyone who
exploits their instincts and impressions: ready to follow, in turn,
today this flag, tomorrow another."

Finally, one must not forget those fictionized paintings of our
reality or a reality to come if the forces at work today fulfill their
course. Though shocking, it is well to read once such books as
Gheorghiu's *The Twenty-Fifth Hour*, Orwell's *1984*, Aldous Huxley's
Brave New World.

[17] David Riesman has given classic expression to what he presumes
may become the dominant type in American society. His "other-
directed" man is one who finds in his contemporaries his source of
direction. His goals shift with the changes in his chosen guidance
(be it through direct personal contacts, or through the mass media of
communication). His behavioral pattern is one of conformity through
means of an outstanding degree of sensitivity to the wishes and actions
of others. Cf. David Riesman, *The Lonely Crowd* (New Haven: Yale
University Press, 1956).

Whyte's popular *Organization Man* depicts a certain facet of
American society with the aim of suggesting a future in which it will
be possible for "individuals" to live as such in an "organization" life.
William H. Whyte, Jr., *The Organization Man* (New York: Simon
and Schuster, 1956).

community grounded upon authentic personal relationships.[18] It is also important to consider what these philosophers single out as the elements in the nature of man which are in danger —above all, human liberty and transcendence through love. Liberty in its dimensions of autonomous decision and self-realization is the distinguishing trait of man, and it is precisely the exercise of liberty which is suppressed in our mass society. Incapable of making decisions, the individual is incapable of asserting himself in his individuality, incapable of swimming against the current of the disintegrating tendencies in himself and in society. The individual, through allowing himself to be absorbed into the mass, eliminates the possibility of true "transcendence" either in relation to others or to God, for this transcendence can be sustained only through the being and activities (particularly, love) of a free person.

With these conclusions from our analysis of the existentialists' critique of modern man, we may now return to the initial thoughts in this chapter. We spoke of the necessity that educational theory should not rest only on a static conception of man—or, in a more general way, on the fixed elements in the *ordo essendi*—but should take account also of its dynamic elements. In examining the situation of man in contemporary society, we have tried to become aware of these dynamic elements, and to open the way for what we will call a time-conditioned view of man capable of providing some enlightenment as to the nature of an educational theory for the twentieth century and the bearing of such a theory on educational practices.

If the situation described in the foregoing paragraphs is a

[18] It must be remembered that emphasis is being laid on the views of Jaspers and Marcel. The possibility of there being a community grounded on personal communication is denied by Sartre's existentialism.

real one, then we must realize that those whom we are educating today, because they are living in a mass culture, will not, in all probability, be wholly free of the traits of the typical man in such a culture. The degree to which they suffer from this contemporary sickness—the pathology of "normalcy," as Erich Fromm has perceptively characterized it[19]—will vary; nevertheless, it will be possible to detect the symptoms in the vast majority of our classrooms, on the college campuses, and in the ordinary give-and-take of community life.

We must be aware that the dissolution of traditional ties in the environment in which our younger generation is growing up—the weakening of family life, the geographical mobility which deprives so many families of the security of a permanent neighborhood, the lack of a core of spiritual values animating the life of the community, and above all the lack of religion— is contributing to the formation of an insecure, lonely type of individual. This kind of individual will be the first to seek security in submerging his individual identity in that of the masses, and, ultimately, as Marcel and Jaspers have pointed out, in yielding to the forces of totalitarian regimes. We must also be aware of the fact that the more mature generation is in much the same danger. Rouault's clown—the image of the lonely, faceless man of today—is, as Thurston Davis suggests, "more of a blood brother than we imagine." A whole set of conditions in our contemporary life "have conspired to produce him, even in the mind and imagination of those whose inner citadel of faith apparently stands firm against so many mammoth irrationalisms. For the impact and resonance of these forces also touch those whose interior life of sanctifying grace

19 Cf. Erich Fromm, *The Sane Society* (New York: Rinehart & Company, Inc., 1955).

thrives somehow even in an atmosphere made heavy by the death of so many ancient sanctities."[20]

A consideration of the dynamic aspects of the *ordo essendi* and of the time-conditioned view of man and community is of importance to education generally. It is of no less crucial importance to Catholic educators, who must recognize (in terms of the principle that human perfection is the result of the action of grace on nature) that the renewal of Christian life, so necessary in a secularized society, cannot be effected unless account is taken of the deteriorated situation, the *actual nature* both of the individual who is to be educated and of those who will become educators.

In his analysis of the situation, Nietzsche, as we have seen, proposed as a solution that we should boldly accept the death of God, and on this postulate reclaim the existence of man in his dignity. But is the restoration of man really incompatible with belief in God? Is it really a question of either/or?—of choosing between the concept of man as a person, fully human and fully integrated with natural reality, and belief in a supernatural God? This is a unique challenge presented to the world of believers, and hence to Christian thought. It is, however, more particularly a challenge to those concerned with forms of education consonant with religious beliefs. It will be their task to prove, on the basis of a new view of man and, closely linked to it, of community, that the depersonalized man and the mass society can be reclaimed not through a rejection of God, but on the basis of a living faith which permeates and perfects nature without destroying it.

To understand more thoroughly the situation we have dis-

[20] Davis, "The Loneliness of Man," *loc. cit.,* 552.

cussed we will examine the position which denies that man can be restored in his dignity in an atmosphere of belief in God and the supernatural world. We will do so in order to grasp the way in which this position has posed the problem, to profit from its insights regarding the solution, and to relate these to the challenge to which we wish to respond: the restoration of man as a fully developed human being in an environment of belief. For this purpose we shall consider the humanisms of Karl Marx and John Dewey.

2

MAN AND SOCIETY IN
THE PERSPECTIVES
OF NATURALISM

THE THOUGHT OF KARL MARX

REFLECTING on the mode of thought of a man to whom he was in great intellectual debt, Karl Marx declared in one of his books that Ludwig Feuerbach's major limitation as a philosopher was his lack of concern with men "under their existing conditions of life," and consequently of "a criticism of the present conditions of life."[1] It is probably true to say that Marx's greatest undertaking in life was to remedy this deficiency and to build up a new world-view on the basis of a critique of society—notably, of man in society.

Marx's thought took shape in contact with the situation of early nineteenth-century society in Germany, France, and England, and it was conditioned by the strong Hegelian influence which in its Leftist interpretation pervaded the German intellectual circles of his time.[2] It was this influence which

[1] Karl Marx and Friedrich Engels, *The German Ideology*, ed. R. Pascal (New York: International Publishers, 1947), p. 37.

[2] The Hegelian Left was a movement which rejected the conservative tendencies of the orthodox Hegelians, who considered Christianity and the Prussian State to be the perfect incarnation of the Idea.

29

provided Marx with the philosophical tools for his reflections on man and reality—the dialectical method and the accompanying concept of "alienation."

Marxist humanism is to a great extent the product of Marx's early years, and for this reason we will confine ourselves chiefly to an analysis of what Marx wrote between the date of publication of his doctoral dissertation, *The Distinction Between the Democritean and Epicurean Philosophies of Nature* (1841), and of the publication of the *Communist Manifesto* (1848). However, social descriptions in his later works— above all, the *Capital*—are of value for understanding the position he took in his first works.

THE CRITIQUE OF PHILOSOPHY AND SOCIETY

Although he started his philosophical career in the Hegelian tradition—that is, in the acceptance of the Idea or Absolute Spirit as the foundation of all reality—Marx nevertheless called attention from the moment of his doctoral dissertation to a danger inherent in this view. He feared that the Hegelian concept of human liberty as only a manifestation of the Idea, and in dialectical opposition to concrete and material reality, meant in practice a separation of the individual from his environment and hindered a practical, transforming action on the world. This goal of changing the world was indeed the aim of a certain group within the wider circle of Left Hegelians headed by Bruno Bauer, which had as its aim the elimination of the irrational elements in the world by means of a rational

---

They expressed the political and social aims of the bourgeoisie, which was rising as a class thanks to commercial and industrial developments. They retained, however, the dialectical method as a doctrine of action. Finding no support in the bourgeoisie, they eventually turned to the proletariat, mainly through Feuerbach and, later, Marx.

criticism of these elements (the philosophy of "criticism"). But a critique divorced from practical action represented a futile attempt in Marx's view. He thus resolved to set in motion a change which would lead to a critique of society, with its philosophical expression, and to a new humanism, but with the addition of a dynamic element which would issue in revolutionary action on the world. He later clarified this aim by making the principle of unity between theory and practice central to his thought.

Two factors confronted the thought of the young Marx. The first was a society in which men appeared to be related, not as human beings, but as objects, or "commodities," in the service of the private interests of a few. The second was a theory which set forth the conditions of an ideal political state in which the general interests would be upheld, a theory, however, which remained in the realm of speculation, without any connection with the real situation and the real political state. This was the Hegelian theory of the state as the embodiment or concretization of the idea.

As chief editor of the *Rheinische Zeitung* (a position which he assumed in October, 1842), Marx began to pay special attention to the political situation of the Germanies; to study the social and economic conditions of the agricultural working-classes, the relations between landowners and tenant-farmers (his debates on the law against the theft of timber and the state of the peasant vine-growers on the Mosel were notable), and to analyze these conditions in the light of the political structure of the Prussian State.

Hitherto, Marx had been an advocate of liberalism in the sense of securing certain liberties from the despotic regime of the Prussian State (an attitude which was strengthened, in its political aspects, with the suppression of his paper by the state). However, his observations of the situation of the land-owners and workers, one group exploiting the other in favor of private interest rather than general interest, now convinced him that the state was no more than an embodiment of this structure of injustice. He realized that it was this conflict between two forms of interest that would have to be resolved —a situation which required measures more drastic than the mere demand for certain liberties.

But there to contend with was the Hegelian philosophy, the philosophy of the German State, which held before the eyes of everyone an "illusory" state supposedly representative of the interests of all. That such a state was an illusion was clear from the fact that Hegel had conceived it not as a predicate of actual social conditions, of the situation of existing men, but rather as an embodiment of the abstract Idea which held man-in-society as its predicate. This was an inversion of reality, a process of "mystification":

. . . Hegel does not conceive of society, the family, etc., in one word, the *moral person,* as the manifestation of the real empirical person, but only as a *real person* who, however, has the element of personality only in an abstract form. For this reason, for him it is not the real person that gives origin to the State, but the State that gives origin to the real person. Instead of considering the State as the highest concretization of the person, as the highest social reality of man, it is *the single,* empirical man, the empirical person, who is conceived as the highest concretization of the State.[3]

While the bulk of men continue to imagine that the state defends their interests, in reality they are being exploited, they

[3] Marx, "Aus der Kritik des Hegelschen Rechtsphilosophie," *Marx-Engels Gesamtausgabe,* ed D. Riazanov and V. Adoratsky, incomplete edition (Frankfurt a. M.: Marx-Engels Archiv., 1927), I, Vol. 1, 1/2, p. 446. (The title of this edition will hereafter be abbreviated as MEGA.)

are being treated by their exploiters (whose interests are the ones defended by the state) as brute objects, not as human beings. They are thus socially, and hence politically, "alienated" from conditions of decent human existence.

In France and England the process of industrialization had promoted conditions which alienated man's human nature still more. The overspecialization of tasks with a view to increased production subjected the worker to a series of unintelligible mechanical functions which maimed him psychologically as he developed a highly specialized dexterity at the expense of his creative powers and impulses. Marx asserted that "not merely are the various partial operations allotted to different individuals, but the individual himself is split up, is transformed into the automatic motor of some partial operation."[4]

Aware of this situation, Marx endeavored to explore all its manifestations, to discover the causes, and to provide a remedy. To this undertaking he brought a previously accepted intellectual and practical commitment. Reared in the liberal atmosphere of a home in which his Jewish parents had become converts to Christianity only for the sake of social acceptance and prosperity, Marx was free of any specific religious beliefs, and because he never underwent the religious crisis common among youth, the religious problem had never troubled him. This enabled him to profess atheism openly in his doctoral dissertation[5] and later on to accept the critique of religion

[4] Marx, *Capital*, trans. Eden and Cedar Paul (London: J. M. Dent & Sons, 1957), Vol. I, p. 381.

[5] Marx stated as the presupposition of his work the following: "Philosophy does not conceal it. The confession of Prometheus: 'In one word, I hate all the gods!' is her own confession, her own maxim, against all heavenly and earthly gods which do not acknowledge human self-consciousness as the highest deity. There must not be any other than him." MEGA I, Vol. 1, 1/2, p. 10.

that Feuerbach had made as well as his reversal of the Hegelian dialectic in terms of a material basis for all reality.

In the light of this attitude, Marx now saw a second form of human alienation, what Feuerbach had called "religious" alienation. Feuerbach asserted that in holding to religious belief man really becomes estranged from his human nature with its own qualities of goodness, truth, love, wisdom, will, and justice, transferring these to a nonexistent being who is a product of his imagination. Marx agreed with this explanation of the origin of religion, but he quarreled with Feuerbach's abstract way of dealing with it, contending that Feuerbach had neglected to consider the real underlying cause of this alienation simply because he had studied it in isolation from the actual, existential condition of men and referred it to some vague notion of the "human species." Marx asserted further that a more drastic remedy for alienation by religion was required than the simple transposition of religion to a natural state of man-worship which Feuerbach was advocating.

What is the real reason that man adheres to a set of religious beliefs and projects his nature outside himself, thereby dehumanizing or alienating his being? In Marx's opinion, this was the result of the social situation. The same cleavage between exploited and exploiting groups in society which deprives men of human reality and leads them to uphold the illusion of a state such as the Hegelian state also leads these men to seek in an alien reality, another "illusion," the human conditions of which they are despoiled in their concrete existence. Religion as seen by Marx is "an inverted world-consciousness," produced by the present position of the state and society:

This State, this society produces religion which is an inverted world-consciousness, because they are an *inverted world*. Religion is the general theory of this world, its encyclopaedic compendium, its logic in popular form, its spiritual point d'honneur, its enthusiasm, its moral sanction, its solemn complement, its general basis of consolation and justification. It is the *fantastic realization* of the human being inasmuch as the *human being* possesses no true reality.⁶

The suppression of religion is a condition for redeeming man, but only a preliminary one. The really imperative need is to bridge the gap between "private" and "public" existence, to advert to the nature of human association. The individual must give up being the abstract citizen of an illusory state and become a member of his species, an individual man "in his daily life and work and situation"; he must recognize and organize that which is his, his *"forces propres,* his own strength, as part of the forces of society, which are then no longer separated from him as a political power."⁷

With these words, Marx was reaching the conclusion that it would be necessary to study, on the basis of the actual situation, that which characterizes man as a unique being, and to develop from this the elements necessary to restore him to his human condition in society. Powerfully convinced, through his experience with the working-classes in Germany and France,⁸ that the status of man in history (concretely, the proletariat, as representing the whole of society) was one of dehumanization, of immersion in the mass structure of a society which had (in its most powerful representatives, the capitalist or

⁶ Marx, "Zur Kritik der Hegelschen Rechtsphilosophie," MEGA I, Vol. 1, 1/2, p. 607.
⁷ Marx, *A World Without Jews,* trans. Dagobert D. Runes (New York: Philosophical Library, 1959), p. 29.
⁸ Marx went to Paris after the *Rheinische Zeitung* was suppressed, and here he began to collaborate actively with the working-men movements, becoming aware of their conditions and feelings.

exploiting class) erected itself into a semi-divine power ruling over functionalized working units, Marx sought for a new humanism. It was to be the stimulus for the revolution which would restore the individual to his human condition, and by pointing out the real distinguishing factors in man, it would clarify the true and ultimate source of human alienation, which Marx could now see as rooted in the economic structure of society.

MARXIST HUMANISM

There were two instruments which Marx utilized in the construction of his humanism. One was, as we have stated, the observation of the social, political, and economic conditions of his times, in which he actively participated in a socialist milieu; the other was his Hegelian heritage. From Hegel, Marx retained the use of the dialectical method for interpreting reality, and possibly a certain sympathy for a sweeping, cosmic vision of reality. However, it is known that in the process of thought which characterized Marx's early years he slowly moved away from the idealism of Hegel, and owing to his continuous regard for concreteness and the material aspects of reality and under the influence of Feuerbach, he ascribed to matter the role that the Hegelian Idea had played in the dialectic. With this equipment Marx began to explain man in terms of a threefold relationship which he observed as proper to human existence: a relationship to nature, to labor, and to society.

The dialectical interpretation of reality is properly an evolutionary one which connotes the three states of: (1) thesis —birth of a being which ultimately will become human; (2) antithesis—self-alienation of this being in the course of historical development; and (3) synthesis—the recovery by this being of his alienated nature and the birth of the humanized man.

On the basis of this scheme, Marx explained that the first moment in the history of man is found in *nature*. This is seen by merely considering the biological constitution of man and its set of drives, tendencies, vital forces—in other words, needs —which are satisfied only in the objects of nature (for example, those providing food and shelter). The satisfaction of these needs contributes to man's being, aiding its consolidation. A closer look at these needs reveals that inasmuch as they push man toward an object outside himself, they are active forces. What man does with these active forces with which he is endowed is to modify nature through the production of some object that will minister more directly to his needs than the object in the raw state of nature. The process is one of the alienation of an individual's proper forces to this product; and it is only when the object is then appropriated by him that the need is satisfied and the alienation redressed. Out of the more simple needs, more complicated ones arise, and with them the origin of certain instruments and tools that will help perform the operations over nature. It is this activity of satisfying more and more complex needs through action over nature—in other words, through *labor*—that is the main factor in bringing human nature into being. It might be said, then, that as man grows he becomes properly human in proportion to the effectiveness of his relations to nature by means of labor —that is, inasmuch as he produces, in terms of his needs, certain objects which he then appropriates for satisfying these needs. World history is in this sense an immense stage on which man, through industry, should be humanizing himself.

But Marx observes also that each individual can only reach

a certain portion of nature, and yet unless this portion can somehow be extended to satisfy all his needs, he will never be properly human. Hence he asserts that production really rests upon *human intercourse* as its essential condition. The needs of one individual may, in certain cases, be satisfied only by the production of another; and this gives rise to labor as a collective enterprise in which "all production is appropriation of nature by the individual within and through a definite form of society."[9]

With this conclusion, Marx gave to the man-nature relationship which labor properly is, a social dimension which he thought it permissible to regard as the chief constitutive factor of man. Because of their need to relate to nature in terms of labor, men join in community, and since they cannot fully realize themselves as men without this association, they are really social products. Man is thus explained not in terms of a disintegrating theory, but of a co-ordinated adaptation of one element of his being to the other through the bond which is society. Marx asserts on this basis that society "is the most perfect unity of being between man and nature, the true resurrection of nature, the realization of the naturalism of man and the realization of the humanism of nature."[10]

This close relationship between society and the human activities of production in its immediate meaning points to a dependence of society upon the mode of production in a given historical epoch. This mode of production in turn is determined by the actual conditions of nature and the opportunities it offers for the satisfaction of human needs. It is the mode by

[9] Marx, *A Contribution to the Critique of Political Economy,* trans. N. I. Stone (Chicago: Charles H. Kerr & Co., 1904), p. 273.
[10] Marx, *Oekonomisch-philosophische manuskripte* (1844), MEGA I, Vol. 3. p. 116.

which the individuals express their life, and Marx adds: "As individuals express their life, so they are. What they are, therefore, coincides with their production, both with *what* they produce and with *how* they produce. The nature of individuals thus depends on the material conditions determining their production."[11]

In the nature-labor-society complexus, the ultimately defining element in man is consciousness. However, consciousness is not something over and above and independent of those relations but is rather their product. It is a state in man by which he becomes aware of his links with nature, of the way he humanizes himself through work and of his dependence upon conditions in social life. Consciousness is the capacity man has for understanding and correctly applying the laws which govern human development in all its relations. It expands and becomes more complex as human needs increase, and since man properly owes his being to the conditions of the social forces, it is true to say that consciousness "is from the beginning a social product, and remains so as long as men exist at all."[12]

Knowledge is a direct manifestation of consciousness. It is a pragmatic activity by which man (on the basis of his understanding of the set of relationships on which he depends) becomes aware of the productive activities which will contribute to the satisfaction of his needs. That is why it is linked immediately to practice, and it brings man-in-society into contact with nature through labor. Practice thus becomes the test of truth, and truth ceases to be absolute and eternal. Considering the meaning given to practice—productive activity over nature—it will be right to say that the conditions

[11] Marx and Engels, *The German Ideology*, pp. 7–8.
[12] *Ibid.*, p. 19.

surrounding productive activity at a certain juncture in history
will determine the standard of truth and the quality of
knowledge.

Morality, like knowledge, is another manifestation of consciousness and is also dependent upon the mode of production
and the social relations involved. In other words, there is no
universally binding law which determines the moral quality of
an action. However, morality exists inasmuch as man is bound
to carry on those activities which accord with the pattern of
the nature-production-society relationship at a given moment
in history. Freedom is simply an assent to this pattern—what
Engels defined as "the control over ourselves and over external
nature which is founded on knowledge of natural necessity . . .
therefore necessarily a product of historical development."[13]

By referring back to Marx's initial critique of man in modern society, we can now approach his meaning of moral action in our times. A proletarian class, a working-class suffering from a form of labor and social organization which
obliged it to devote long hours to an increasingly mechanized
type of work (as in the industrial centers of Great Britain),
and to live in indescribable conditions of poverty, sickness,
and ignorance, was the symbol of a dehumanized or alienated
society. This factor clarified the real nature of the political
and religious alienation Marx had already detected in society. Inasmuch as the humanity of man depends ultimately
upon the conditions of production, the actual situation could
only be explained as a distortion in the understanding of these
conditions, that is, as presenting some contradiction in the
economic structure of society. Such was the case of the
capitalist or bourgeois society, as Marx saw it. This society

[13] Friedrich Engels, *Anti-Duehring,* trans. Emile Burns and ed.
C. P. Dutt (New York: International Publishers, 1939), p. 125.

had organized itself in contradiction to the factors regulating the mode of production. History revealed how, with the appearance of exchange and division of labor, productive activities had become collective, bringing the individual to an equivalence with society and demanding that he produce and appropriate as a collectivity. However, the capitalist society, far from recognizing this fact, had established a division between production (in the hands of the mass of the population) and appropriation (in the hands of the few owners of the means of production). This division kept the individual worker permanently alienated and dehumanized, since he could never obtain the return of his product or even see it and appreciate in it the expression of his own productive powers.

Where such a situation prevails—that is, where a society, by a misapprehension of the nature of productive activities, sets up a false structure—then all other types of alienation ensue: a social alienation (through class division), a political alienation (the contradiction between the sphere of "private" individual existence and "public" existence), a religious alienation (the projection of the desire for a life worthy of a human being onto an imaginary entity which represents all that man would wish to be).

In the light of the above conditions, the moral imperative becomes clear. If, owing to economic conditions, political and social life present factors alienating to man, one must try to counteract these forces and work for the realization of man in the fullness of his human dignity. To create "a new man," a wholly integrated individual, entails seeing him as a product of the social situation in which man-in-society (a collective) alienates himself to the product of his labor, and then, through receiving it back (collective appropriation), reunites in himself the elements in nature, labor, and society which constitute him.

Marx gave classic expression to this moral imperative in his appeal for an overthrow of the existing conditions of society (the emancipation of the working-classes as representative of the emancipation of humanity as a whole), and the establishment of a new communist society. In this society, a correct interpretation of the meaning of labor and property would resolve all conflicts between man, nature, and society:

> *Communism* is the *positive* abolition of *private property,* of *human self-alienation,* and thus, the real *appropriation* of *human* nature, through and for man. It is, therefore, the return of man himself as a *social,* that is, really human being, a complete and conscious return which assimilates all the wealth of previous development. Communism as a complete naturalism is humanism, and as a complete humanism is naturalism. It is the *definitive* resolution of the conflict between man and nature, and between man and man. It is the true solution of the strife between existence and essence, between objectification and self-affirmation, between freedom and necessity, between individual and species. It is the solution of the riddle of history and knows itself to be this solution.[14]

Summarizing what has been said about Marx, we may repeat that he was vitally aware, through experiential contact with his society, of the degraded condition of the working-man. He was witnessing the development of the industrial era and could observe here the danger of the mechanization of the individual human life. He drew conclusions from this situation, conclusions which were greatly colored by his Hegelian background and the influence of Feuerbach. To rehumanize man it was necessary to reinterpret the nature of man in terms of the fundamental set of relations in which he is involved, and once a clear understanding of this is achieved,

[14] Marx, *Oekonomisch-philosophische manuskripte,* p. 114.

to work practically for the establishment of those conditions (economic, social, and political) which would give birth to a real man. Marx understood man to be the result of the social activities of production-in-nature, and on this basis he drew the picture of the future communist society which was not to be distinguished from the new communist man.

The social dimension in man and the mystique of the new society are elements in Marxist thought which have received a special emphasis in the Russian interpretation of the Marxist theories. It is perhaps well to consider briefly their communist man and society in order to become aware of the direction to which these two elements in Marxist humanism may lead.

It is a basic principle in the Russo-communist interpretation of Marx's humanism that if man is entirely a product of social relations (which of course link him through labor with nature), then the only human reality is that of the collective society they have established and seek to consolidate more and more. In this direction, one of the authorities on Russian communism has declared that "communism understands by 'man' the *collective*," and that as such, the individual "exists only as a 'moment' of the 'whole' . . . of society."[15]

Resting on the dialectical view of reality (which received its classic expression from Engels rather than Marx himself), the collective society is seen as an entirely self-created entity which arises from nature in virtue of the inner dynamism of matter.[16] Religion is combated not only because it is unnecessary, but also because it obscures the consciousness of

[15] Joseph M. Bocheński, "Zur Kritik des Kommunismus," *Handbuch des Weltkommunismus*, eds. Joseph M. Bocheński and Gerhart Niemeyer (Freiburg-Muenchen: Karl Alber Verlag, 1958), pp. 636–637.

[16] This inner dynamism is explained through the classic laws developed by Engels and restated by Lenin: the law of the struggle and unity of opposites, the law of negation of the negation, and the law of transition from quantity into quality by "leaps."

their nature and origin which men need in order to develop
as "free" individuals who assent to their collective existence.

This collective society, thanks to an emphasis on the ideological superstructure[17] which stems not from Marx but from
Stalin,[18] is conceived as the supreme norm of truth, morality,
and culture, and makes its decisions in this respect binding
for all. This situation is valid both for the society intermediate
between the capitalist and communist one (the dictatorship
of the proletariat) and for the final communist society. In the
first case, one organism in the social group assumes leadership, an organism which theoretically is the representative of
the majority. In the second case, all distinctions being abol-
ished, the whole coincides with the organism of the transition
society. This organism is today the Communist Party, whose
dominion extends to everything: political and economic problems, law, questions of nationality; the arts and sciences, religion, the spiritual life, and the most private affairs of man.[19]

The individual in this collective society has no reality of his
own, since he is theoretically a product of society and its
economic forces. The identification of man with society and
with nature, which is strengthened by Stalin's stress on the
interconnectedness of all phenomena in nature (including
man), leaves no room for a concept of individual reality nor,
consequently, for individual responsibility and self-assertion.

[17] This is the realm of consciousness, freedom, ideas, that Marx
made dependent upon the underlying economic conditions.
[18] Cf. Joseph Stalin, *Dialectical and Historical Materialism* (New
York: International Publishers, 1940), p. 22. Gustav Wetter states
that Stalin's emphasis on the "organizing, mobilizing and transforming"
significance of the superstructure is restated clearly in Kruschshev's
Report to the Twentieth Party Congress, stating that, especially with
regard to communist idealogy, there will be no condescension to
"coexistence." Wetter, *Dialectical Materialism*, trans. Peter Heath
(New York: Frederick A. Praeger, 1958), p. 220.
[19] Cf. Bocheński, "Die formale Struktur des Kommunismus,"
Handbuch des Weltkommunismus, pp. 13–14.

Individuals are respected only insofar as they produce for the collective society, and not for any intrinsic worth. The individual becomes a function of a great human machine, a means to the purposes of this machine. His uniqueness, his reality as a person, must fade, since it is conceived as something derived from the collective; and thus, where the individual is concerned, personality is effaced.

Today communism is an ideal that attracts many. It may be, as Wetter suggests, that this influence is possible because the doctrines underlying the entire system of dialectical materialism (that matter is the only reality, and that the world has come into being "of its own accord") conform to the views of a great majority of the world's population.[20] However, it is also true to say that communism relies for its attraction upon the basic aim of Marxist humanism: to save man in his present condition from a process of dehumanization to which the forces of society are subjecting him.[21] Because of this it is all the more important to make it evident that communism attempts to save humanity by crushing the individual and by eliminating all factors which point to his uniqueness; that consequently it does not now fulfill, nor does it contain the promise of fulfilling in the society of the future, Marx's aim of restoring the individual's integrity, simply because the individual is not conceived as a human reality apart from the collective. This flows from the Marxist principles themselves (reinforced, of course, by the developments in Russian thought before and since the Revolution)—notably, the total identification of the individual with society, and

[20] Wetter, *op. cit.*, pp. 548–549.

[21] In no other way can the attraction of communism be explained when attention is paid to the masses of people living in inhuman conditions—in some areas of Latin America, for example—who rapidly yield to the promises of a better existence which are expressed by communist leaders.

through it with nature and production, even in his distinctive conscious activities. Thus, though the day may come when economic conditions in the new society are such as to take from everybody according to his ability and give to everybody according to his needs, the individual will still be little more than a well-adjusted part in the mechanism of the society. He will have had to give up, as Ignace Lepp, a former Marxist, holds, "the right to look at himself, to pose questions concerning his own destiny, concerning the ultimate meaning of his existence and the final end of the human collective."[22]

Marx did not conceive of this annihilation of the individual's reality as an aspect of his future society, but it is implied in his definition of man in terms only of a nature-labor-society relationship with the exclusion of any distinctive element, transcending nature, whereby man could have remained independent in being and could yet have acknowledged these relations—which are, in truth, important factors in his mode of existence.

Whatever the intention behind Marxist humanism, Russian communism today attempts to prepare the way for a new communist society as the supreme collective reality for all men. Among its means, it has paid special attention to a transformation of man through education in order to make him receptive to and disposed for the future collective society.

It is of interest to follow briefly the lines of the educational structure of today's communism in order to see in what ways they remain faithful to the basic commitment to the communist society.

Underlying the emphasis on education is Marx's dictum: "if man is formed by circumstances these circumstances must

[22] Ignace Lepp, *Le Marxisme: Philosophie ambigue et efficace* (Paris: Librairie Editions Labergerie, 1949), p. 293.

be humanly formed."[23] Practically, this means that education will assume the task of providing the environmental influences by which man may develop in his relations to nature, work, and society, and by which he may grow into these relations without conscious awareness or a commitment to do so.

If we look at the aims of communist education, we can say that inasmuch as the collective society is the entity which expresses all the relationships in which man is involved, then it is clear that to form the social man, the man who will perfectly fit into the new communist society, is the ultimate goal. In this respect a communist educational theorist in East Germany has stated: "The entire moral formation and education must lead our students to develop into men who think and act collectively, who consider as their own the success and happiness of the collective, who joyfully contribute their part and cooperate steadfastly in the higher development of the collective."[24]

Looking at the means by which this general aim may be fulfilled, we can see that on the basis of the identification of the individual with society, all social contacts are considered as educational. With this in view, attention is paid, along with formal schooling, to such institutions as the family, youth organizations, and propaganda.

Education must start from the very early years of the child's life if it is to have a transforming effect. In this respect, Soviet educators have moved more and more toward a recognition of the importance of the family. In faithfulness to the Marxist principles, the family is conceived as the community of work-

[23] Marx, *Die heilige Familie*, MEGA I, Vol. 3, p. 307.
[24] Gertrud Schroeter, ed., *Didaktik* (Berlin, 1956), pp. 21 ff. Quoted in Gerhard Moebus, *Psychagogie und Paedagogik des Kommunismus* (Koeln und Opladen: Westdeutscher Verlag, 1959).

ers where it is possible to find the most closely-knit set of production-relations. Thus Soviet education asserts that it is in the family that one finds the cradle for those sentiments, the "feelings of social sympathy," which are essential to the new society. According to Anton Makarenko, one of the prominent Soviet educators, a child who is reared apart from a father and mother has no experience of those feelings of filial love which must be later transformed into feelings of patriotism, the highest human feeling in the communist society.[25]

Early in its life, the child is sent to nurseries and kindergartens (which exist in every industrial, commercial or business center) where, through poems, tales, songs, and games, the children are brought into contact with the persons and institutions of the Communist Party.[26]

The eight-year compulsory general school in Russia has as its aim to educate the new man in his fundamental defining

[25] Moebus, *op. cit.*, pp. 22–23.

[26] The following translation of a poem (a secularized church song) which a child has to learn in East Germany illustrates the manner in which he is conditioned to see all the joy and beauty in nature and life as a gift from the "great Father of the German Democratic Republic," the symbol of the "new society": "Games and songs and books; sports and a happy time; birds that fly, sun and stars and moon; clouds and wind and sea; and the home of spring—these are all things we love so well. Fields and woods and prairies; and the nice baked bread; and the running spring; and the morning red; cats and dogs and horses; and the cattle moving gently down the slope; and the deep brown earth; all this is for us to enjoy. Everything is given to us with plentiful hand; dream and sleep and peace, and a fatherland; we give thanks for a colorful and beautiful life, for the rich joys of childhood, to the efforts of our Republic; and to the white-haired man on the steer, who is our intelligent, good and faithful father." "Der Kinder Dank," *Schulpost* (October, 1955); quoted in Moebus, *Mitteldeutsche Jugend als Gesamtdeutsche Aufgabe* (Koeln: Die Heimstatt, 1956), pp. 30–31.

activity, work, in order to build the collective society economically and "to bring up the youth in the spirit of profound respect for the principles of socialist society, in the spirit of the ideas of communism."[27]

The educational ideal of forming the new man who thinks and acts collectively is carried out by emphasizing such accepted expressions as respect for the life and dignity of men, love for man, for the home and the fatherland, love for the mother tongue, love for order, cleanliness, punctuality, self-criticism, self-control, etc. They are presented as ideals in the context of lectures and discussions which form part of the educational methods and which are authoritatively guided by the teacher. But they are presented together with the basic tenets of communism so that their validity is seen as deriving from the fact that they reinforce these tenets.

Youth organizations, the Pioneers for children between nine and fourteen years of age, and the Komsomol for those between fourteen and sixteen, complete the work of the family and the school in permeating the life of the growing child with the principles and ideals of communism. This is further reinforced by means of propaganda. Kulski, one of the students of communist methods, has declared that wherever a communist turns—to his pamphlet or book, radio or television, a public lecture or a class in the university—he always has to contend with the restatement, in all wave-lengths, of the "Party line."[28]

Education would not be complete unless special attention were paid to what Khrushchev has called "the engineers of the

[27] "1958 Educational Law," art. xi, sec. 2; quoted in Elizabeth Moos, *Soviet Education Today and Tomorrow* (National Council of American Soviet Friendship, 1959), p. 12.

[28] W. W. Kulski, "Die Situation des Individuums," *Handbuch des Weltkommunismus,* p. 618.

soul of the young generation," the educators. This training for teaching in secondary schools is given at Pedagogical Institutes or universities, and in order to insure a clear grasp of the Marxist principles, a sizable portion (one third) of their entire program is spent on communist ideology and history.

Education is definitely at the service of the new communist man and society, and it attempts not so much to indoctrinate directly (though this is an integral part of their objectives), as to create an atmosphere in which the child from his early years learns to think, not in terms of his own observations and reflections, but in function of a collective consciousness; and in the same way, he is taught to evaluate his actions only in terms of their public repercussions or their equivalence to the acts of society as a whole. The result, in the mass of the population at least, is an individual who accepts whatever the dominant tone of the "Party line" is. Religion has been eliminated from his life so that no alien disturbing force may cause the individual to deviate from the established form. Hence we have an individual who has reality only in the collective, who believes this to be his only reality, and who fights for this belief.[29] How closely this situation resembles that of the depersonalized man in Western society whom existentialists have criticized can be determined by reflecting on the constitutive elements of the depersonalized man which have been presented in the introductory chapter: surrender of the capacity for independent reflection and personal decision and subjec-

[29] A group of members of the Comparative Education Society reported, from their 1958 visit to the Soviet Union, that the moral education based on conformity to a set of rigid rules set by communist dictation, to which children and youth are subjected, is leading to a submersion of the individual in society and endangering, as a consequence, the essence of humanity. Cf. George Z. F. Bereday, et al., eds., *The Changing Soviet School* (Cambridge, Massachusetts: The Riverside Press, 1960).

tion to the trends of "the majority" outside the individual's self. This is secured by eliminating all forms of personal, spiritual rootedness in persons, land, objects, ideas, work, and God—and by supplying the obvious need for roots through a collective society (including its smaller units, notably the family) and a collective ideal: to work for the consolidation of this society in which the individual finds security by losing himself in the whole.

THE THOUGHT OF JOHN DEWEY

It was the American intellectual, social, and economic structure that for the most part conditioned the philosophical outlook of John Dewey. During the long span of his life he witnessed the enormous changes brought about by the application of empirical science to industry and technology, and the movement from a simple form of social life (such as was typical of his native Burlington, in Vermont) to the complex life in the great industrial centers, the overpopulated cities with all their problems. He underwent the impact of Hegelian thought as it was received in America by William Torrey Harris and the Saint Louis School of Philosophy, and then, while retaining some Hegelian elements, he moved to a form of philosophical naturalism conditioned by the Darwinian discoveries, the pragmatic philosophy of James and Peirce and, more immediately, by the social philosophy of George Herbert Mead.

It was society that troubled Dewey, and, most of all, man in American society. He examined the effects of the growing industrialization at the turn of the century—the development of immense social groups in which the man who until yesterday had been a person accepted and respected as such in his small home town was now lost, unaware of the complicated structures rising above him. Thus Dewey spoke of the "lost individual" in a constantly increasing intricacy of social, political, and economic mechanisms. An external expression of this situation was a growing attitude of conformity which Dewey described in terms similar to those of the existentialists:

We think and feel alike—but only for a month or a season. Then comes some other sensational event or personage to exercise a hypnotizing uniformity of response. At a given time span, taken longitudinally, instability and flux dominate. I suppose there are others who have a feeling of irritation at such terms as "radioconscious" and "air-minded" now so frequently forced upon us. I do not think that the irritation is wholly due to linguistic causes. It testifies to a half-conscious sense of the external ways in which our minds are formed and swayed and of the superficiality and inconsistency of the result.[30]

Men were conforming because of a real lack of understanding of the new social forces and conditions. The individual vaguely aware that something is happening, but not of why and how it is happening, experiences fear and insecurity. This is strengthened when he finds that his fellow-men are in the same predicament. Dewey asserted that in the absence of a common mentality congruous with the new social corporateness, a community of understanding, the individual yields to whatever force may offer some substitute for this lack. Such can be, for example, the suggestions coming from propaganda. Dewey then interpreted conformity as "the artificial substitute used to hold men together in lack of associations that are incorporated into the inner dispositions of thought and desire."[31]

[30] John Dewey, *Individualism, Old and New* (New York: Minton, Balch & Company, 1930), p. 85.
[31] *Ibid.*, pp. 85–86.

A situation such as this cannot be cured by means of a restatement of tenets similar to those of the individualism of the past centuries, since all such a conception does is to establish an insurmountable dualism between the individual and society, a solution that can never be effective for a time in which the category "social" has a far greater resonance than ever before. What is needed, Dewey asserted, is to become aware of the existing situation (a society in which technological and industrial developments generate conditions of life which may ultimately dehumanize man) in order to evaluate it properly. It will be necessary to formulate, on this basis, a "way of life" which can be shared by all, and which expresses existing social forces. And Dewey added: "the sick cannot heal themselves by means of their disease, and disintegrated individuals can achieve unity only as the dominating energies of community life are incorporated to form their minds."[32] The main effect of this "way of life" will be to release individuality for creative effort, an effort which in turn will reflect upon society, allowing it to be ever renewed and fresh.[33] This was Dewey's personal task.

Two factors in the contemporary setting required special attention: the constant change which the technological age and its discoveries was projecting over society, and the growth of the urban population and improvement of communications which were bringing people closer together. In this condition it was imperative to dissolve the age-old dualism between the individual and society, and to discover the means by which men could feel at home again in a world of change. Dewey sought a solution for these problems by pointing to what he considered the source of the individual-society dualism and

[32] *Ibid.*, p. 65.
[33] Cf. *Ibid.*, p. 143.

by reinterpreting the constitution of reality in order to provide
an explanation for change. And both these approaches he
united in a naturalistic conception of reality.

In his interpretation, Dewey was aided by his Hegelian
background, which had left impressed upon him the notion
of a unifying world-view capable of overcoming such dualisms
as the split between the individual and society. He explained
that Hegel's thought "supplied a demand for unification that
was doubtless an intense emotional craving [on his part] . . .
Hegel's synthesis of the subject and object, matter and spirit,
the divine and the human, was, however, no mere intellectual
formula; it operated as an immense release, a liberation."[34]
However, it was ultimately the Darwinian world which shaped
Dewey's thought and provided the basis for his metaphysics
(which he defined as cognizance of "the generic traits of
reality"). Dewey attributes to Darwin the liberating action of
opening a way for submitting the study of human reality to
the procedures of empirical science, and for explaining
change.

On the basis of an evolutionary view of reality, Dewey
explained the genesis of the dualism between the individual
and society as the consequence of a much deeper dualism,
the one between nature and supernature. Our world is one in
which there is a "mixture of sufficiencies, tight completeness,
order, recurrences which make possible prediction and control, and singularities, ambiguities, uncertain possibilities,
processes going on to the consequences as yet indeterminate."[35]
In the midst of this world characterized at the same time by

[34] Dewey, "From Absolutism to Experimentalism," *Contemporary
American Philosophy,* eds. G. P. Adams and W. P. Montague (New
York: The Macmillan Company, 1930), II, p. 19.
[35] Dewey, *Experience and Nature* (Chicago: Open Court Publish-
ing Co., 1929), p. 47.

stability and precariousness men search for security. However, instead of acting upon the world in order to modify it and place it at the service of human ends, they have set up against it an imaginary world, a world of immutable reality in which they hope to find the desired security. It is the realm of supernature—a world of eternity, omnipotence, infinity, and immutability in contrast to a world of finitude, weakness, limitation, and change.

On the basis of such a dualism it is easy to interpret all the unstable elements in reality in terms of further dualisms. The dualism between man and nature is a result of the belief in something in man which links him to the supernatural realm (his "spiritual soul") and separates him from nature, which is inferior and unstable. In practice, this induces man to live in two worlds, the actual and the ideal. When tortured by the irreconcilability of the two, man flees his environment, escapes tiresome responsibilities, and withdraws into his ideal world. But also, he compensates "the strains of renunciation involved in membership in the ideal realm by pleasurable excursions into the delights of the actual."[36]

The dualism between man and nature justifies all currents of individualism inasmuch as it emphasizes individual consciousness—an inner private life—neglecting actions with public meaning and a consideration of man in his social relations.[37] This is the source of the dichotomy between the individual and society which is menacing the integrity of human life.

Resting on his Hegelian heritage—the notion of the possibility of a unifying cosmo-vision—Dewey asserted, in the

[36] Dewey, *Human Nature and Conduct* (London: George Allen & Unwin, Ltd., 1922), p. 8.
[37] *Ibid.,* p. 86.

spirit of the Darwinian discoveries, that behind the mixture
of stability and precariousness in all reality lies its evolutionary character, its continuous movement and change. William
James' psychology had earlier affected Dewey's view of the
human mind and helped him to see it only in a biological context; now with the possibilities opened up by the Darwinian
investigations (and, closer to home, by social Darwinism,
which was popularized in America through the lectures of
John Fiske at Harvard in 1869–1870), he found a justification for his assertion that the human mind—the characteristic
distinguishing the human being—is only a product of evolution; that it is an activity differing not in kind but only in
degree from the lower activities of matter. Thus the concept
of a spiritual soul is ruled out. Given the conflict in reality
between the stable and the precarious, every organism must
develop means of adjusting to this situation. It is in this way
that the human mind comes into being as an instrument for
resolving existing conflicts. Finally, it was George Herbert
Mead, the great sociologist who worked with Dewey at the
University of Chicago, who showed Dewey how the dualism
between the individual and society could be overcome entirely
by submitting to philosophical naturalism. Mead's contention
was that mind is an evolutionary product which represents the
culminating point of social activity.

With these elements in mind, we may now look at the
picture of man that Dewey presented.

In the great realm of nature, all individual existences are inserted in a system of connected events in which they find a
secure milieu; however, at the same time, each individual
existence is in conflict with its surroundings. In order to resolve
their discordances with the environment individuals come into
relation with each other, they interact. This is something that

is always going on, but on different planes. For example, there is a physical field of interaction in which we find all non-living things emerging and consolidating themselves through reciprocal contact; then there is a psycho-physical level where we find a type of interaction between living things which gives rise to such new elements as "sensitivity" and "feeling" typical of plants and animals. Finally, there is a level at which life is dominant in a unique way: there emerges an instrument which allows the individual, in unity with other individuals, to perceive a meaning in nature, and on the basis of this meaning to direct his energies toward a transformative action upon nature. This instrument is mind, and its possessor is man. The type of interaction that has developed here is what we call "communication," and it is conditioned by the set of signs and symbols known as language. Communication is the totality of shared perceptions of meaning, or "consciousness" of meaning, which appear in the "workings of organic life."[38] I become really human when I am able to work out in union with others and benefiting from what others have done, a set of hypotheses which serve as possible ends or consequences for my actions of control over nature. This creative power of communication makes it "the greatest of human goods,"[39] something to be valued both as an end and as a means, and therefore with moral signification:

Because of its characteristic agency and finality, communication and its congenial objects are objects ultimately worthy of awe, admiration and loyal appreciation. They are worthy as means, because they are the only means that make life rich and varied in meanings. They are worthy as ends, because in such ends man is

[38] Dewey, *Experience and Nature*, p. 303.
[39] *Ibid.*, p. 202.

lifted from his immediate isolation and shares in a communion of meanings.[40]

The fact that man is a product of communication, or of socially shared experiences, makes him dependent upon the given state of society. We can never understand man apart from a consideration of the forces at work in the social group to which he belongs. The "actions and passions" of individuals, including their beliefs and purposes, are what they are "because of the social medium in which they live."[41] In other words, the factor to be recognized is that social forces are the means by which individuals are created.[42]

The human self is constituted by the social context from which it emerges; nevertheless it remains essentially an active self which in turn reacts upon this context. Thus the problem of conduct—the interaction of the individual with his environment—is important. Conduct is to be conceived both as shaped by the community and as sufficiently creative to react on this community, conferring new forms upon it. These actions are performed with the use of the scientific logic of inquiry which allows for the development of intelligently controlled actions. Dewey means by "intelligence" a function and an instrument which allows me, as an individual, to perceive on the basis of my social relations the possible consequences of an action and to determine thereby the truth or goodness in it. As a result, thought is never isolated from action,[43] and morality, or the problem of conduct, remains the essential

[40] *Ibid.*, p. 205.

[41] Dewey, *The Public and Its Problems* (Chicago: Gateway Books, 1946), p. 195.

[42] Dewey, *Reconstruction in Philosophy* (Boston: Beacon Press, 1949), p. 194.

[43] In his antidualistic efforts, Dewey sought a unity between theory and practice, knowledge and action, as much as did Marx.

concern of man. No ultimate or fixed ends regulate conduct; there are only those ends-in-view (the anticipated consequences of an action) which we are able to perceive in the context of inquiry or moral deliberation. However, there is a sense in which one can speak of a certain "direction" which guides moral actions; this is the promotion of those conditions which are properly human—namely, the growth in the communication and sharing of activities. Community is built upon communication; the ideal community, the "great community" as Dewey calls it, is the community in which every individual shares in the results of inquiry and knows the consequences of the activities carried out in common. This ideal is specified by the concrete circumstances in which the community finds its embodiment, and being the ideal of community, it is at the same time the ideal of man, who in himself is born from and molded by society. Such an ideal, for our times and especially for American society, was characterized for Dewey by the word "democracy."

Dewey had asserted that only an awareness of the forces at work in society and the embodiment of this awareness in a common "way of life" or life-outlook could save man from the dehumanizing process to which the dichotomy between the individual and society and an irrational control of man by his own technical discoveries might subject him. With the aid of philosophical naturalism Dewey reached an understanding of man in terms of his links with nature through society, and with this he hoped to provide for man a view of reality which would make him understand, and feel at home in, a world of ever increasing changes. All of Dewey's philosophic reflections were based on his study of the main forces at work in his society, and when he came to express them in one ideal, the democratic ideal, he was really trying to provide the "way of life" which he envisaged as saving the humanity of man.

Underlying the meaning of democracy is the notion that there are such things as goods (above all, moral ideals and values) which endure only by being communicated, and that association is the means which makes possible such communication. Dewey asserted that "communication, sharing, joint participation are the only actual ways of universalizing the moral law and end."[44] Democracy has no fixed meaning. Its meaning appears in the context of the historical circumstances of society, and that is why it is able to respond to a rapidly changing society as characteristic of our century. Nevertheless, the notion of "democracy" serves as an ideal—that is, an element which in spite of its changing structure could provide a basis of security for man in his contact with a reality fraught with peril, both in nature and in the human community.

The meaning of democracy as an ideal finds one of its clearest expressions in this passage.

Regarded as an ideal, democracy is not an alternative to other principles of associated life. It is the idea of community life itself. It is an ideal in the only intelligible sense of an ideal: namely, the tendency and movement of some thing which exists carried to its final limit, viewed as completed, perfected. Since things do not attain such fulfillment but are in actuality distracted and interfered with, democracy in this sense is not a fact and never will be. But neither in this sense is there or has there ever been anything which is a community in its full measure, a community unalloyed by alien elements. The idea or ideal of a community presents, however, actual phases of associated life as they are freed from restrictive and disturbing elements and are contemplated as having attained their limit of development. Wherever there is conjoint activity whose consequences are appreciated as good by all singular

[44] Dewey, *Reconstruction in Philosophy,* p. 206.

persons who take part in it, and where the realization of the good is such as to effect an energetic desire and effort to sustain it in being just because it is a good shared by all, there is in so far a community. The clear consciousness of a communal life, in all its implications, constitutes the idea of democracy.[45]

As the ideal of community life, democracy is at the same time, and for this reason, the ideal of individual life. The belief in man as a product of the forces of society, or rather of their communicating activities, really means faith "in human intelligence and in the power of pooled and cooperative experience." It means that the individual can grow and can "generate progressively the knowledge and wisdom needed to guide collective action."[46] In the final analysis, democracy is the upholder of the dignity and worth of the individual independent of any necessity of disjoining him from the reality of his associations. Democracy is, in this way, the solution to the dualism between the individual and society which generates the conditions for dehumanization. It is an ideal that can be understood both from the standpoint of the individual and of the community. From the standpoint of the individual it means a "responsible share according to capacity in forming and directing the activities of the groups to which one belongs and in participating according to need in the values which the groups sustain." From the standpoint of the group, it means "liberation of the potentialities of members of a group in harmony with the interests and goods which are common."[47]

Democracy as the ideal of the individual and of community life offers to those who believe in it the fruitful qualities of a

[45] Dewey, *The Public and Its Problems,* p. 149.
[46] Dewey, *Problems of Men* (New York: Philosophical Library, 1946), p. 59.
[47] Dewey, *The Public and Its Problems,* p. 147.

religious experience inasmuch as such experience involves an attitude toward any object pursued as an end or ideal. This ideal, however, to generate religious experience must be continuously tested against the changing circumstances; this is what makes the ideal actual, and in the last analysis, what makes it valuable for human life. To believe in this "active relation between ideal and actual" is to believe in God, is to give meaning and security to life in a universe devoid of the imaginary belief in a supernatural God:

A religious attitude . . . needs the sense of a connection of man, in the way of both dependence and support, with the enveloping world that the imagination feels is a universe. Use of the words "God" or "divine" to convey the union of actual with ideal may protect man from a sense of isolation and from consequent despair or defiance.[48]

The ideal democracy is thus one which has its being in an active relation with the actual as expressed in the give-and-take of human relations. The concept of democracy is at once an ideal and the object of this ideal. It is an ideal in that it suggests the attitude of promoting communication and sharing. It is its object in that in itself it embodies this process of communicating. It further remains an ideal in that its very meaning connotes continuous adaptation; it is the one thing that we see always in process and yet not really changing. That is why democracy corresponds with Dewey's conception of God, and that is why it calls for "religious" experience. There is also a sense in which one can speak of a "religious" faith— namely, the faith in the possibilities of "patient, cooperative in-

[48] Dewey, *A Common Faith* (New Haven: Yale University Press, 1934), p. 53.

quiry operating by means of observation, experiment, record and controlled reflection."[49]

Summarizing what has been discussed up to this point, we may say that Dewey viewed man as a being generated or created by the mode of association in which his biological existence develops—in other words, the type of society in which he is born. As he is created by the community, he is also endowed with creative activity by which he can act and contribute to the growth of the community. The need of a meaning for his life as well as for a goal of action capable of engaging all his energies defines the ideal of democracy, gives religious quality to his experience, and allows him to find the security needed in a precarious world in democracy experienced as "divine."

But these conditions are not given gratuitously. They must be worked for. It is necessary, then, to examine the nature of social relations as they exist in our times. In particular, it is necessary to become conscious of the mode of association and the activities and values which flow from it. These will be the determinants of our cultural forms. To reach this awareness, the individual must be consciously molded in relation to the dominant culture in its positive aspects—concretely, the democratic culture. It is society that can perform this task, the whole human community and every small community in which the individual finds his existence. The community will have to see that the special values and special purposes of the democratic society "receive such distributions that they become part of the mind and the will of the members of society."[50] This process can be accomplished most effectively by *education,* the instrument which society has for generating

[49] *Ibid.,* p. 32.
[50] Dewey, *Problems of Men,* p. 37.

those members who will enhance its values and contribute to its growth. And, in this light, Dewey made education a central concern of his life and intellectual activities.

THE EDUCATIONAL ENTERPRISE AT THE SERVICE
OF THE DEMOCRATIC IDEAL

There is in Dewey's thought a deep connection between his view of man and education. It is not simply the normal connection we find everywhere between education and human development; it goes beyond it to suggest a *creative* relationship. To understand this statement we must like Dewey conceive of education as the means whereby a society transmits its structural form; since men are generated within and through this social structure, it would be legitimate to assert that education is a process creative of man. It is at the same time the institution that guarantees the existence of society inasmuch as it preserves the dominant social forms and simultaneously develops the creative faculties in man so that he can act in a transforming way on society. Its ultimate aim, in other words, is the reconstruction of society without destruction of its essential elements.

It is in terms of Dewey's concepts of the continuity of man with nature and of the social dimension in human existence that we shall now examine some of the elements in his educational theory.

Man is an evolutionary product of nature, and thanks to his distinguishing trait, mind, he is in continuous interaction with nature. The human mind allows man to find meanings in nature which direct his actions. This interaction between man and nature (including social reality) is what Dewey called "experience." In these terms, education is a force which acts upon man, stimulating his mind and actions so that he can assert himself in nature and society and receive, in turn, influences which stimulate his growth as a being in nature and society.

The educational task consists mainly in selecting those experiences in the environmental context of the child (natural and social) which will best promote a balanced and full growth. However, the child's role is not one of a passive reception of certain stimulations, but rather one of active participation in the process of experience (in conformity with its meaning of interaction). In other words, the child learns by doing; the curriculum is not simply an arrangement of dead subject matter but consists, on the contrary, in an active relationship of the child to certain stimulations (the necessary material of knowledge). This is the main theme that Dewey developed in his *The Child and the Curriculum*.

If we consider further that the human mind is an instrument which grows out of nature and improves in the measure in which its instrumentality is put to use for the perception of meanings in nature (thought) and the actions which follow, we see that it is only through activity that the child can learn to think. Intelligence is the ability to formulate possible courses of action to be pursued when faced with a problematic situation—an interruption in the interaction between the individual and the environment—and to anticipate the consequences that may flow from such actions. This is a function to be developed, and it can be done only through activity. When thinking is understood in this way, it is clear that the same logic which governs the experimental sciences can be used to resolve any problematic situation: we consider a situation, formulate an hypothesis, experiment or act upon it, and then, on the basis of the consequences, decide whether our theory was true and our action good. The experimental scientific method is the all-important method for developing in the child his capacity for thought, but it does not imply concentration on physical or muscular activities only. It simply means that mind works the same way in relation to every object, and that whenever a child observes something that disturbs him and seeks to clarify his problem by some activity, he has really perceived a meaning and an anticipated consequence and has acted upon his perception (knowledge and practice firmly united). In theory, the curriculum should be as wide as the whole of nature, since nature is the child's environment; however, Dewey asserts that in fact there must be selectivity. This selection is to be made in terms of what best promotes human growth at a certain moment and in a certain situation, and for this purpose of selection we may use empirical scientific methods, as for everything else. In the same line, if we consider that human nature is not fixed and that education makes a positive contribution to its development, then we see the infinite possibilities that are open. Education must devise, with the aid of scientific inquiry, those methods which will best serve the development of man in the direction of a balanced growth.

In terms of Dewey's concept of mind and of the importance of scientific inquiry, *discipline* becomes a state whereby the child, on the basis of intelligent deliberation, sees the need for certain actions rather than others as helping him to grow in his experience. In this sense there can be no opposition between freedom and discipline. Freedom in its true meaning is "freedom of intelligence," that is, "freedom of observation and of judgment exercised in behalf of purposes that are intrinsically worthwhile."[51] Dewey wanted to make clear that he was

[51] Dewey, *Experience and Education* (New York: The Macmillan Company, 1938), p. 69.

not advocating a total freedom such as sometimes did appear in the classrooms of "progressive" schools. There should be freedom of outward action, but only to serve as a means to freedom of judgment and of power to carry out the chosen ends.

The social dimension in man is, as we have seen, the factor that ultimately justifies Dewey's position on education. He saw the whole of society as one great educational institution, but he concentrated, in his theory, on the school as the most important single agency for the transmission of the values of the community and the formation of its members.

The school must become a "miniature community" where the type of culture dominant in the greater community can find a living expression. In the school the child must learn to become a member of his society, but he must also learn how to preserve and modify it. The atmosphere of the institute is the first means for this purpose. Inasmuch as social life implies the sharing of experience, the school should be characterized by the activities of co-operating individuals and not by the authoritarian atmosphere in which a dictator presides over little silent "receivers." If intelligent activity and thought find their full expression only when conceived as social activity, then the atmosphere of the school, the methods and materials employed, should be such as to provide for the incorporation of the child into the life of the community. That is why emphasis will be placed on activities typical of the particular community to which the children belong. *The School and Society,* for example, was an expression of the needs in the society at the turn of the century. The activities Dewey proposed here were designed to restore to the child living in an urban society the primitive contacts with the elements which had contributed to the building of such a society, and which otherwise the child would never experience. That is why the child was not simply taught to use a basket, he had to know how to weave it, where the materials it was made of came from, how these materials were extracted from nature, and so on. These activities were not designed to train the child for any calling, but rather to keep him in contact with the processes that were giving life to his society. Of these activities Dewey said:

We must conceive of them in their social significance, as types of the processes by which society keeps itself going, as agencies for bringing home to the child some of the primal necessities of community life, and as ways in which these needs have been met by the growing insight and ingenuity of man; in short, as instrumentalities through which the school itself shall be made a genuine form of active community life, instead of a place set apart in which to learn lessons.[52]

The traditional arts and sciences which give content to the curriculum are there in a new form. The occupations in which the child is employed are to provide the basis for drawing their historical, social, and scientific premises and equivalences.[53]

Generally speaking, the school must bring the children to an active participation in the life of the community: "the only way to prepare for social life is to engage in social life."[54] For this aim to be fulfilled, the prerequisite is a clear knowledge of the community in which the school operates, and the school

[52] Dewey, *The School and Society* (Chicago: Phoenix Books, 1959), p. 14.
[53] *Ibid.*, p. 22.
[54] Dewey, *Moral Principles in Education* (New York: Philosophical Library, 1959), p. 14.

itself must further contribute to this knowledge through its activities. In its all-embracing form, the school in twentieth-century America is to enhance the democratic society—that is, the society in which democracy as a "way of life" dominates, in which every mature human being is to participate in the formation of the values that regulate human association, something required for the general social welfare and for the full development of human beings as individuals.[55]

To adhere to the ideal of "democracy" as Dewey envisaged it means that the democratic faith will substitute for the supernatural religious faith lacking in the Dewey school. All the means of education—methods, curriculum—will serve to confirm the individual in this faith. The teacher is to realize "the dignity of his calling," which is to transmit and preserve the democratic ideal; he must realize that "he is a social servant set apart for the maintenance of proper social order and the securing of the right of social growth." In every way, the teacher is always "the prophet of the true God and the usherer in of the true kingdom of God."[56]

It was undoubtedly a very acute perception of the situation of man in American society which was the origin of much of Dewey's philosophical speculations. As we have seen, he was conscious of the necessity of a humanism capable of responding to the vast changes wrought in society by industry and technology. He realized that men needed to obtain some intellectual hold on the phenomena occurring around them, that they were searching for a secure milieu in face of this vast sea of experience which threatened to engulf them. Particularly, Dewey saw the need for re-examining the question of human relations in

[55] Dewey, *Problems of Men,* p. 58.
[56] Dewey, *My Pedagogic Creed, Education Today,* ed. Joseph Ratner (New York: G. P. Putnam's Sons, 1940), p. 17.

a society that was bringing great masses of human beings externally closer, but with no guarantee that this external unity would either produce or maintain a communion of understanding and co-operation. In many passages, Dewey beautifully presented an ideal of community life based upon balanced and creative human relations, a true human love.

It was this awareness that the problems presented by the new structures in society were deeply rooted in a displacement of man (a separation from nature—the mechanization of work —and a loneliness in the big social mass), that guided the formulation of Dewey's new humanism, his view of "democracy" as a "way of life." However, Dewey limited his study of man precisely to man in his natural and social relations. He made a study of man in his biological and social dimensions, interpreting human reality in terms of the Darwinian universe.

In order to preserve in man a certain uniqueness and to account for the conscious or spiritual functions underlying intellectual activities and such experiences as those of art and religion, Dewey utilized the social factor, the capacity for interaction at the level of communication. He saw man's distinguishing trait in his ability to perceive meanings in nature and communicate these to his fellow-men, and he saw the mark of man's freedom in the recognition of this ability. However, by asserting that the only method for dealing with man was the method of empirical science, that is, of physico-biological reality, Dewey treated man as if his conscious elements were nonexistent.

Dewey's conception of thought as a socially-conditioned entity endangers, in practice, the possibility of that creative action upon society which Dewey himself desired. If action is to be creative, it must be the product of a form of thought that transcends the immediate social milieu. An individual educated

to see in his social environment the whole of his possibilities
of realization will be able only with difficulty (and a high
degree of intellectual endowment) to step back and evaluate
critically (even in terms of the scientific method, as Dewey
counseled) the forces at work in his immediate surroundings.
The mass of the people will simply yield to the dominant forces
of social communication which they have been taught to see
as "the greatest of human goods."

If the mode of thinking and feeling of the community is to
be that of the individual, then the community itself must be
the embodiment of all that is seen as typical of the worth and
dignity of the individual. This Dewey fully granted when he
asserted that the community is made up precisely by a concrete
association of human individuals, and when he gave this
meaning to his ideal community, "democracy" as a "way of
life." However, if there are only ends-in-view, short-sighted
goals dependent upon the given environmental conditions, and
determined by a method that virtually excludes the treatment
of man in his distinctive functions, it is difficult to see how the
relation between the ideal of the community and the situation
of the individual is to be always preserved without degenera-
tion. The time may come when individuals, accustomed to
see in the stream of social life an embodiment of their own
being, may submit their freedom of action and their responsibility to a social organism which, forgetting that it owes its
origin to an association of free individuals, may seek to impress
these individuals into the service of some set social purpose.
And perhaps this is not far from collectivism.

In terms of the foregoing, we do not see that man as a
person, a reality distinct from his relations to nature and
society, is either clearly presented or guaranteed in Dewey's
humanism. Where man's distinctiveness as a thinking being is

dealt with only by methods which apply to non-thinking beings, and where in his distinctiveness the individual is made to be wholly dependent upon social relations, it is difficult to preserve a principle by which man can relate and yet be able to transcend these relations—that is, can avoid losing himself within them. Hence we fear that in spite of Dewey's very different intention, he has provided the basis for a dehumanized or depersonalized theory of man. We have seen, through our brief survey of Dewey's views on education, the extent to which his theory colors his assertions in this field. We know further that his educational principles have had a definite impact upon society, though not always in the way he would have wanted. However, where the social dimension of education is concerned, it is probably true to say that Dewey's views have been thoughtfully considered and applied for decades in American society and beyond it. On this basis, we might have reason to suspect that the depersonalized situation of man, in its essential traits (loss of creative and free individuality in face of the mass structures in society),[57] has not been corrected by this education, but has probably been reinforced by it.

We must acknowledge, and we do, that the impact of Dewey's thought upon education has brought about many salutary effects both in theory and practice—notably, the accentuation of freedom and spontaneity in education and of inner controls of behavior as opposed to external disciplinary methods. We also acknowledge that the basic orientation toward stressing the role of the individual in his relations to nature and society is sound; nevertheless the premise that this social reality is

[57] We refer here to the descriptions presented in the first chapter, and especially the recent research of sociologists and psychologists on the conditions of man in contemporary society.

the only reality the individual has, according to which he must be educated, makes us declare that Dewey's education carried to its fullest consequences will not help our modern uprooted mass man to find *his* individual place in nature and society.

SOME THOUGHTS ON THE HUMANISMS OF MARX AND DEWEY

Though acknowledging that they are genuinely concerned with the situation of man in a society characterized by new forces of development which threaten human disintegration, we have endeavored briefly to indicate that the naturalistic humanisms of Marx and Dewey offer no real solution to the problem. In the case of Marx, we find that the identification of man with his productive forces conceived in a social context has guided the developments which Russian communism has brought about today. These developments in practice, by submerging the individual in the collective, have not saved him but have on the contrary functionalized him and virtually suppressed his existence as a person. This cannot be maintained with regard to the consequences of Dewey's humanism. Nevertheless his approach to man is essentially the same as Marx's, and therefore he interprets man only in terms of natural and social forces. Dewey, like Marx, has dangerously compromised individual existence, creativity and freedom by leaving to the social forces at work in a man's environment his entire formation, and by neglecting to provide for any private, individual reality transcending these forces. Practically conceived, these theories, when active educationally, have no power of improving the condition of man, of making him feel at home as an individual in the world and in society. Not only do they not

improve the situation, they reinforce it through their impact.[58]
In this light the picture which existentialist philosophers drew
for us, and which we described in our first chapter, appears
with clearer contours. The problem is more acute since even
those who are aware of it are not really providing a solution.[59]

Nevertheless the social critiques and theories of Marx and
Dewey have approached the problem and hit on important
phases of it in a way which is, in our opinion, of value for an
understanding of man in his present condition.

In the first place, these theories were based on observations
of a political, economic, and social reality. They started with
a critique of the wholly abstract character of other humanisms
and stressed the necessity for getting down to actual conditions.
They also called attention to the place of man in nature and
society and to the links existing between them. Dewey in
particular realized that the new forces of technology, mass
production, urbanization, social organization, the communications media, etc., were bringing about the disintegration of
the former simple bonds of man with nature, making him an
easy prey to the increasing complexity they produced in society.

Secondly, these theories placed emphasis on what we might
call a "psychologizing" or "subjectivizing" of these relations of
man with nature and society by asserting the need for a social
environment or community in which the individual could
almost unconsciously come to conceive of himself only as a

[58] It is known that these theories are strongly influential in Western
society. It is particularly in parts of Europe and Latin America where
economic and social conditions have been most adverse to the mass of
the population that Marxism has had its fruits, while Dewey has left
a definite mark in the United States.

[59] We abstract from the existentialists' solution which we have not
examined in detail, but which as yet is not influential enough in the
practical order to be able to suggest its effectiveness.

part of nature and society. This idea was contained both in the communist and the democratic theories of society and was to be realized, in the first instance, by revolution and education, in the second mainly by education.

What these theories have accomplished is to put us on notice that we cannot, in our way of dealing with man, remain aloof from cultural developments. They remind us that we must acknowledge man as a being of relations and recognize the importance of social forces for his existence. They point to the vital necessity of re-establishing the individual in a life of genuine community. They have demonstrated in an unmistakable way that in face of the danger of dehumanization which a complex of social conditions poses, we cannot resort to an unqualified condemnation of these forces, which in themselves can be channeled for the good of society. Nor can we move back, when faced with the danger of a mass society, to a unilateral individualism. On the contrary, we must find the means by which man can live in modern society without losing his reality as a human being. Finally, whatever the conclusions one reaches regarding man's situation and the possible remedies for it, our experience of these humanisms should make it clear that our own relations will have to move out of the realm of theory to a concrete actualization in widening circles of the human society. This, it seems to us, is the true import of the mystiques of "communism" and "democracy"; the one principle that has so impressively guided the theories we have studied: the unity between theory and practice.

Most important is the fact that they have emphasized *one* of the interpretations that can be given to the modern situation of man: that religion, by apparently failing to evaluate the natural conditions of human life, has dealt with man as an abstraction, has generated false dualisms in his life or justified

alienating social and economic conditions, thereby contributing to his dehumanization.[60] In these terms they propose to
give their assent to the movement that seeks to eliminate
religion and to redefine and redignify human reality by rein-
tegrating and absolutizing man in nature and society. This
absolutization of man is to provide the basis for human security which the elimination of religion puts in peril.

The solution proposed by the humanisms we have been
considering makes more peremptory the challenge presented
in the closing paragraphs of our first chapter: to show that
the dignity of the human person can be restored in an atmosphere of Christian belief. If we are to meet this challenge
objectively, it will involve acknowledging the natural relations
and attitudes which give meaning to man and support to faith
and undertaking to rectify the disintegration in this natural
basis with the ultimate aim of showing that a fulfilled human
being is possible only in a context in which nature and supernature are integrated as perfectly as possible.

In meeting this challenge the believer must take as his
starting-point the realization that while man's being depends
on the net of relationships which integrate him with nature
and society, he cannot be fully equated with these relations,
that to do so effaces his uniqueness as a human person.
Practically, this means that a basis must be provided on which
man can be linked to nature and society not only by productive activities or social-scientific experimentation but also by

[60] It is of importance to note that the rejection of revealed religion
in Marx and Dewey, was conditioned to a certain extent upon the notion of God derived from Hegelian thought and which they conceived
as depriving man of his natural traits and relations. It was also conditioned by personal circumstances: Marx, by a family liberal in religion; and Dewey, perhaps, by an extremely authoritarian type of
religiosity as the one in which he was brought up.

bonds of an internalized nature (knowledge and love) which do not compromise his being. To reinstate this basis means ultimately to transcend the boundaries of naturalism and make way for a return to God as the necessary being who sustains a contingent being in a real, though participated, act of existence, and as the reality which can explain the elements in human life that naturalism evades, such as sorrow, sickness, and pain.

The task ahead can now be seen in a more meaningful context as we realize that the situation of the depersonalized man and mass community depicted in the first chapter is only reinforced by the practical impact of theories which conceive of man as absolutized in nature and society. We have, then, a stronger reason for placing emphasis on the need which a form of education that recognizes the reality of the supernatural has of acknowledging the situation of man. In concrete terms, we must make a place for a *lived* Christianity in a society which tends to deny theoretically and/or practically the existence of God.[61]

This task presupposes a search for the means by which the individual can learn to live with and utilize the new developments in a novel and constructive way without destroying himself and the community and, consequently, the necessary natural basis for the work of grace. We must find the ways by which man can connect his faith in God with the persons and ideas, activities, things and places upon which he by his nature

[61] Of interest in this respect is the statement in Pope John XXIII's social encyclical, *Mater et Magistra:* "It has been claimed that in an era of scientific and technical triumphs, men can construct their civilization without God. But the truth is that these same scientific and technical advances present human problems of a world-wide scope which can be solved only in the light of a sincere and active faith in God, the beginning and end of man in the world."

depends and which he needs in order to be fully human. And at the same time the criteria must be provided by which he can critically evaluate the areas in which he finds depersonalizing forces, forces which endanger the vitality of Christian life.

As Dewey and Marx realized, the problem of man cannot be solved without an awareness of his distinctive traits in terms of his present situation. Hence, before concentrating on the task of Catholic education, we shall pause for a few reconsiderations of man in his nature and existence. This will be done in the light of the thought of some present-day Catholic philosophers and theologians.

3

MAN IN A
CHRISTIAN PERSPECTIVE

THE PROBLEMS dealt with in our first chapter and in our conclusions to the chapter on naturalism have provided a double orientation for the treatment of man we propose to undertake here. First of all, we have noted the existence in modern man of a marked trend toward conformity, toward an inability to assert himself by firm decisions and consequent action. We have seen him as yielding increasingly to the "majority" in society and in his group, and as making his way of thinking and acting dependent on the direction of these trends. On the basis of the existentialists' social critique we have become aware of the ominous resemblance between modern man in the free society of the West and the member of totalitarian states who is forcibly made to feel, think, and act as the state or its society dictates without recognition of his freedom and, hence, of his uniqueness.

Secondly, we have perceived the connection between this situation of man and the developments in science and technology, the movement of urbanization and industrialization, the immense growth of communication media—all of which have, in many cases, contributed conditions for what the existentialists term the *uprootedness* of modern man. Marx and

Dewey had already seen that if man lacks a vital connection
(that is, a connection which is felt and experienced as a part
of the self) with those elements in nature which he needs for
his existence, and above all, with society, he develops in a
fragmented way and is consequently prone to lose awareness
of his total being, of his humanity. Uprootedness, as the existentialists describe it, is the phenomenon of man deprived to
such an extent of the contacts natural to his existence, and of
the feeling of participation in them, that he comes to experience himself as an insecure "something" floating in a vacuum.
To attain some semblance of security, he holds onto whatever
substitute satisfaction for his natural needs he finds available,
and in our time this substitute is the mass culture and society.

These two aspects of the problem—the depersonalized man
and the mass society and the uprooted condition of the individual which is their source—pose two urgent tasks for our
epoch.

In the first place, we must take account of what we will call
(not in any pejorative sense) the movement of "collectivization" in our world. In itself, it is a natural development from
the constantly increasing complexity of society produced by
the geographical expansions of the fifteenth and sixteenth
centuries and the rise of modern science. Inasmuch as it
corresponds with man's social nature, it is a movement full of
possibilities for good.[1] However, in our times, it is in danger
of being fatally wounded or at least badly deformed, and this

[1] Such possibilities are viewed by Teilhard de Chardin as enabling
the universe as a whole to complete its process of evolution, which is
the convergence of all mankind in God, the Omega of the universe.
This movement includes intrinsically a development in the direction
of personalization. Cf. Pierre Teilhard de Chardin, *The Phenomenon
of Man*, trans. Bernard Wall (New York: Harper & Brothers Publishers, 1959).

danger constitutes the crux of the modern problem. The person, the free unique individual who should give meaning to the movement of collectivization, is being forced—either by state authority or by uprooting factors in society which he has not been able to interpret or survive—to yield this uniqueness. Hence the need, as we have seen, of redirecting the stream of collectivization to its proper bed, one that can never annul the reality of the individual.

If we assert that it is a dissolution of natural ties that lies at the source of man's insecurity and his surrender to the mass, then these ties must somehow be restored. For this, however, we must understand the meaning of man in these terms; we must take a look at this being which we call man, penetrating a little beyond the merely phenomenological in order to grasp how and in what sense he is able to achieve individual integrity as a being-in-relation. If we are able to do this, then we have a starting-point for the direction that the practical solution should take (an effort which, as we see it, must be in some way paralleled in education).

These, then, are the two guidelines that will direct us. Acknowledging the existence of a trend toward deformation in the collectivization or socialization movement of our times, and aware of its connection with the condition of the natural ties which we normally see as belonging to human nature, we will try to look at man in his meaning and existence.

THE MEANING OF HUMAN NATURE AND EXISTENCE

Human existence as it appears in our experience is an existence interwoven with that of other beings; it is a situated existence, an existence which is bound to a place and a time, and which draws upon its environmental conditions. We need to feel that there are things which belong to us, that we have a home, a country; we need others from whom to receive and to whom to give, we need them in order to communicate our ideas and experiences and to make theirs our own. We are characterized, as a whole, by physical and psychological needs which necessarily bring us into contact with what exists outside ourselves.

However, our experience also discloses moments in which we somehow stand above these natural ties, though in no absolute sense; they are the moments of choice, of decision, of assertion of our selves. They are moments in which a combination of circumstances leads to reflection, to decision, and to action; they are moments of a choice which moves beyond the present instant, and which comes into being because of some value we have made a part of ourselves. These experiences make us aware of being something other than a factor in a world of relations, of somehow being unique.

Thus we see man from two angles. There is, on the one hand, the fact of his dependence upon a material reality—on nature, its elements and products, and on society. But there is also in man the capacity for self-assertion on the basis of an individual decision which, though taken in his relational situation, places him over and above this situation. It issues from the power man has of becoming reflectively aware of his ties and of ordering them for the good of his being.

The above distinction between what binds man to the rest of the material world and what sets him apart from it brings us to the concept of the "human person," or the factor which defines man as an autonomous individual. And this factor, as we observe, resides in the human power of reflection and love and in man's freedom.

A number of philosophers in the Christian tradition have consistently adhered to Boethius' definition of the person which sees the spiritual or rational element as the defining feature of man.[2] However, as the concern with the existential status of the human person increases, and as the failure of one-sided rationalistic views of man to provide a sound foundation for moral life becomes evident (we refer principally to humanisms in the idealist tradition), it appears more and more necessary to integrate the understanding of the person with the understanding of man as a being in a context, an incarnate reality, an embodied spirit.[3]

It is in this sense that we see the value of Mouroux's characterization of the human person not simply as a "subsistent individual of a rational nature," who is independent and incommunicable, but as a being "who is simultaneously spirit and body, closed and open, existent and yet to be achieved."[4] What is of most interest to us here is the person's subsistence, or closed reality, and his openness.

Subsistence is the quality that man has of existing in his own right, the independence in being which makes him a reality that cannot be identified with his relations, a being that

[2] St. Thomas, *Summa Theol.*, 1.29,3 quotes Boethius: "Person signifies what is most perfect in all nature—that is, a subsistent individual of a rational nature."

[3] The weakness of the idealist humanisms was brought to the fore by the early critiques of Marx, Dewey, and Kierkegaard; and today this critique is upheld by some currents in Christian philosophy which are precisely attempting to understand man as an incarnate being. Notable examples are Marcel's existentialism and the French Personalist movement.

[4] We should like to remind the reader that our concern is not first of all to justify the metaphysical formal principle of man, in which case Boethius' definition should be stressed, but to accentuate what the person really *is* in his present condition: a form substantially united to matter.

exists in himself, by himself, and for himself.[5] It means further that as such, the individual possesses his being and orders his existence to his own good, the good of his being. In other words, the person exists as a reality sealed off from his environment, a unique and irreplaceable individual with a value and an end wholly his own.

But the person is also *open*. He is a being who transcends himself and who is capable of projecting, from that very center which makes him subsistent, a new life into the bonds with nature and society that are a part of his incarnate existence. Through the activities that flow from this center—knowledge and love—the person is able to incorporate the outside world, thus enriching his existence; and, at the same time, he is able to communicate outside of himself something of the richness of his own being. In this way he adds to those relations upon which he depends a new spiritualized or interiorized dimension.

This openness of the human person rests, as we may suspect, upon the fact that he is also a closed reality, upon the fact that there is something in his being which preserves his individual existence and avoids total fusion with the world to which he is open. And this core of his being requires in turn some principle of subsistence which cannot be any of man's material objects of dependence or other men; since, even though they are conditions for his physical and psychic well-being, they limit human existence and, if too absorbing, they threaten its independence. The principle that sustains the person as a closed reality must be free from such limitations, and this leads us to recognize the metaphysical bond that links the human person to Him who sustains him in being and as-

[5] Jean Mouroux, *The Meaning of Man,* trans. A. H. G. Downes (New York: Sheed and Ward, 1952), p. 118.

sures for the person a closed or independent existence in the midst of his openness. In this sense we say that the human person is open in a new and different dimension: open to God. We come to acknowledge that we can exist as independent beings, even though fully linked with fellow-beings in our own order and others below us, because our being is dependent on, and participates in, a Being who is the fullness of all that we value in the person and is able generously to communicate His perfection to us and sustain our independence by His own fullness and subsistence. We come to acknowledge that the human person, because he is a whole and unified center of being, is at the same time open, metaphysically open, to God; and participating in His perfecting activities of knowledge and love, he is able to give to his human ties the new and enriched forms of which we have spoken.

With this, human existence is seen in its third dimension. We find ourselves born in nature and depending upon it as well as on our species. We further become aware of ourselves as transcending these relations, as somehow above them with a reality that is all our own and which becomes a center of activities that links us in a new way to our world of relations. And yet we realize at the same time that we are not fully independent, that our own reality is somehow linked to a greater and higher reality which is the fullness of being, and that it is in virtue of this reality that we preserve the worth and personal dignity which no other one of the objects of our relations is able to assure for us permanently. Thus we find that although as subsistent beings we have a closed existence we are also open to God, the source of our being and of our personal subsistence. And thus we need not relate slavishly to the world which nourishes our material existence, for in Him in whom we have our being we are able to communicate

generously of ourselves and to receive from outside that which
enhances our being, but without destroying it—in other words,
we are able to stand above the limitations of our human mode
of existing in relation.

The perfection of the human person cannot be fully understood in terms of a perfection in the exercise of the activities
which define him as a unique being; the appeal to the third
dimension is necessary. However, this appeal which, as we
have presented it, rests on the metaphysical structure of man
is deepened and illumined in a new way when we bring to
bear upon it the facts of Revelation. It is then that the fullness
and beauty of the human person appears related to an entirely
new order, the supernatural order. In this light we see how
the three Divine Persons of the Trinity furnish the highest
exemplar of our reality as persons and, by supernatural grace,
make it possible for man to participate in the divine reality
which is its source. For man is in the first instance by nature
sustained in being as singular and unique by his creation in
the image and likeness of God, and by grace he participates
in the nature of God. And this active participation issues in
the communion of man with God as a son with his father.

This brings us to the essential factor in the elucidation of
the meaning and perfection of the human person: man's active
participation in the being of God is possible only in his likeness
to, and communion with, Christ, so that ultimately his uniqueness resides in his Christlike character, in the perfection of
his whole human nature by the saving gift of Christ.[6] The deep
meaning of our union with Christ is to bring us, in the power
of the Holy Spirit, into a living relationship with the Father,
not only as creatures who owe to Him our being, but as
children, adoptive children; and this relationship is, in the last

[6] Cf. *Ibid.*, pp. 134–135.

instance, the august mark of our humanness, the quality by which we are brought into the stream of divine life and are able to participate in the personal reality of God.[7]

Recognizing that the meaning of the human person in its ultimate connotations involves his insertion into the supernatural order, and that his full dignity lies in his real and active participation in the being of God (his divine sonship), we must now return to man, the natural and supernatural man, and contemplate from this all-embracing angle his existential or temporal integration in God, and thus the movement toward the realization of his personal reality.

What has been said up to now really constitutes a static image of what man is by nature and what he is called to be by grace. However, in his concrete existential state man is not simply a *given* reality, but also a reality *in becoming*. While we can speak of a metaphysical human structure and of the effects of grace upon this structure, we must acknowledge that here and now man is moving toward the realization of that being which his structure marks for him. Hence we have man as a dynamic reality striving for his perfection, and we ascribe this dynamism to the moral order. As Maritain has said, what the human person is by nature is merely a sketch of what he must become by vocation.[8]

What meaning does this striving for perfection have for man? Considering the nature of man and the world of his relations, it is possible to define it with the single word "integration"; it involves the harmonious and hierarchical unifica-

[7] Cf. Matthias Joseph Scheeben, *Nature and Grace,* trans. Cyril Vollert, S.J. (St. Louis: B. Herder Book Co., 1954), pp. 116–149.

[8] Jacques Maritain, *The Person and the Common Good,* trans. John J. Fitzgerald (New York: Scribner's Sons, 1947), p. 34.

tion in man of his various powers and activities, and the harmonious and hierarchical union of man (though with preservation of the self) with what exists outside of him and above him. This is what one writer has termed the quest for a "structural" and "functional" unity in man.[9] Let us now see what it means more concretely.

To understand the dynamism of man we must examine his *activities*. Here we find in man a twofold sphere of activities: those which belong to his organic nature—those he shares with the animal—and the rational activities which define him as a person. At each level these activities are seen in two dimensions: cognitive and appetitive.

At the organic level we have the sensory knowledge which is the ground of rational or conceptual knowledge, and we have the sphere of sensible affectivity which strengthens and provides the basis for spiritual affectivity and, more immediately, for love. The function of the rational forms of knowledge and love, in their reference to the organic activities, is to incorporate them, order and place them at the service of human ends. This is the process of self-integration which plays such an important part in the movement of human perfecting.

Even though at this point we shall, for the most part, confine ourselves to the consideration of human nature, we should see it in relation to the new dimension that comes to raise it and lead it to its final perfection. The rational integration of the sensible spheres by the intellect is further perfected in the same order by faith, and the elevation (without destruction) of sensible affectivity by love is led to its completion by the supernatural virtue of charity. The task, then, of integration which man must carry out in his lifetime culminates with his incorporation into the supernatural order; and this integration,

---

[9] René le Trocquer, *Homme, qui suis-je? Essai d'anthropologie chrétienne* (Paris: Librairie Artheme Fayard, 1957), p. 121.

aided by grace, is accomplished in the measure that the natural
basis is sufficiently strong to serve as the ground of the action
of grace; in other words, grace perfects, but does not super-
sede, nature. A closer view of the meaning of the natural and
the supernatural in man, and of the relations between these
two orders, will aid our understanding of the human way to
perfection and the applications we will later make to the
process of education.

The natural is that which pertains to our nature, to its
essence. It refers to our body and soul with all their powers:
reason, will, imagination, sensibility—all, in fact, that makes
up the human composite—and to the activities which flow
from them; and it includes the natural ends to which our
activities are directed. Our nature also takes in the whole of
the universe of which we are members and to which we are
related. This universe was envisioned by St. Thomas as a
harmonious and organic order in which the less noble creatures are designed for the more noble, creatures lower than
man are designed for man and both are designed for God.[10]
Man as a microcosm incorporates in himself the order of the
universe and the organic relations among the members of this
order, so that we are able to speak of human nature as a
natural organism.

The supernatural, on the other hand, pertains to the elevation of man to a higher order in virtue of a gift of God which
is totally distinct from his nature, which exceeds all his natural
capabilities and potentialities, and which comes to inhere in
his nature as an accident. And just as the natural order in
man is an organic one (he is, as we have said, a microcosm
incorporating the order of the universe), so also the supernatural order appears as an immense organism, "a great *mystic*

[10] "The order among the members of the whole is possible because
of the ordination of the whole to God." St. Thomas, *De Pot. Dei,* 7.9.

cosmos erected, out of the depths of the divinity, upon the world of nature."[11]

The relations between these two organic orders is not simply that of one order being placed next to the other, but rather of a radical elevation and incorporation of the whole order of nature into a higher realm. Supernatural life modifies nature "so deeply and affects its inmost being and essence so powerfully that the limits of possibility are reached."[12] Both orders then come to exist in us in an integrated organic relationship without the order of nature's being annulled by the supernatural life. Grace itself *presupposes* a natural foundation; it rests immediately on the natural ability to know and to love, but as a whole it rests upon the integration of every one of the human powers, ranging from the senses to the faculties of the spirit. Grace also *perfects* this nature, and it does so in five ways: (a) it awakens and harmonizes all human powers in a unity which is superior to the human composite; (b) it grants equilibrium to all human tendencies; (c) it perfects the natural virtues; (d) it allows for the beauty of a divinized humanity to appear through the small efforts of mortification and self-denial which are called for in daily life; (e) it adapts itself marvelously to the natural temperament of the person, thus allowing for perfection in all his natural gifts.[13]

In a general way, we may say that the two orders are related to one another (keeping in mind the hierarchical ordination of one to the other) as means of expression, of protection, and of help. For example, the natural love of a

[11] Matthias J. Scheeben, *The Mysteries of Christianity,* trans. Cyril Vollert, S.J. (St. Louis: Herder, 1958), p. 18.

[12] Scheeben, *Nature and Grace,* p. 30.

[13] Cf. Francis Hermans, *Histoire doctrinale de l'humanisme chrétien,* Vol. IV: *Esquisse d'une doctrine* (Tournai-Paris: Casterman, 1948), pp. 90–94.

child by its father *expresses* or mediates the paternal love of God for man, and the child, by loving his father, learns to love God; on the other hand, the filial love of God by grace gives to the natural form of filial love its highest expression. This same relationship *protects* the meaning of divine sonship inasmuch as it serves to exemplify for the child the nature and qualities of the paternal love of God; on the other hand, grace protects this natural love from becoming egoistic and deviating from its source and meaning in divine love. Finally, the natural love of a child for its father, including all the affective factors, *helps* or gives renewed strength to the child's love of God as he sees Him in his own father; while grace helps this natural and instinctive love to mature and become permeated by charity.

With this we come to realize that the task of full integration of all the natural activities of man ultimately requires the help of grace: proximately, however, if a solid natural foundation for the action of grace is to be laid, the sound exercise of the activities at the natural level is required. And it is to the meaning of these activities and their links with the supernatural virtues that we will now turn.

The contemporary trends in Catholic studies on human nature reveal a renewed interest in human liberty (as the expression of the rational activities of the intellect and will), and, in a special way, in love.[14] From our consideration of the elements in the problem of modern man and community

[14] An example is the treatment of the human person in Mouroux's *The Meaning of Man,* which centers human activities around spiritual liberty and love, and Christian liberty and charity. Our treatment of liberty here, unless otherwise specified, follows largely Mouroux's treatment. It is also of value to note the works of Marcel, and the personalists, the late Emmanuel Mounier and Jean Lacroix for example, on the subjects of liberty and love. In the same order is M. C. D'Arcy's *The Mind and Heart of Love* (New York: Henry Holt and Company, 1947).

(a depersonalized man who surrenders his power for self-assertion and a mass society which is a herding of men by means of purely extrinsic links), the importance of these studies becomes evident.

Human *liberty* in its dimensions of choice or decision and of action is an expression of the defining powers of the person (intellect and will), and because of this, it is properly the instrument for human self-realization. We find, first of all, that free acts are always acts of the whole person in view of their very constitution. They rest on the intellect's capacity for judgment and on the will's inclination toward good and the possession of good. One cannot say that the subject of liberty is either the intellect or the will; it is always the will in its relation to intelligence[15] and both in their interaction.[16] But freedom is above all man's instrument for self-realization. All the individual's choices and decisions constitute an assertion of his being and are capable of leading in the direction of increased perfection. However, because of the actual state of man[17] a wounded liberty is also capable of leading him in the opposite direction—toward enslavement. Man can become the victim of his passions and irrational impulses instead of achiev-

[15] St. Thomas, *De Veritate*, 24.4,10.

[16] Cf. Gérard Gilleman, S.J., *The Primacy of Charity in Moral Theology*, trans. William F. Ryan and André Vachon (Westminster, Maryland: Newman, 1961), p. 106.

[17] We refer here to the fallen state of human nature, which affects the integrity of the human activities and the harmonious ordination that should exist between them. We know, of course, that nature is not intrinsically depraved, but that only the way of man to his ultimate end is hurt; we know also that redemption has opened a gate for a final surpassing of the actual disorder in nature and for our incorporation in God. We must remember, however, that we remain fallen and redeemed creatures who must constantly follow the way of Christ to achieve our perfection: the way of the cross, but of a cross that is love.

ing the integration of these into his spiritual powers. In these terms, one must conceive of a movement of liberty which leads to enslavement and of one which leads to self-fulfillment— which is ultimately the true meaning of liberty. Both are movements of integration:

> . . . spiritual liberty is reached at the end of a long effort of integration—the corporeal, affective, and spiritual powers being re-grouped, unified, and orientated towards the gift of oneself which shall perfect the person. Spiritual servitude represents a like integration in the opposite direction—the same powers are unified for that self-refusal which makes men "carnal."[18]

The real meaning of liberty, however, cannot be conceived only in terms of its choice-dimension; rather it must be seen in terms of the individual's capacity for harmonizing his activities in the direction of self-fulfillment by means of an enlightened knowledge of what constitutes human perfection and of the strength of a will ready to work for this perfection.

In his analysis of liberty, Mouroux points out that free acts (in the widest meaning of freedom, as choice) can be seen under a double light. They may be acts which confirm or prolong an existing condition or acts which create a fresh dimension of freedom. The first case is exemplified by the individual who throughout his life has come to organize his various habits, emotions, feelings and inclinations, his voluntary choices, around a certain end. This end is what Mouroux terms a "dominant inclination," one which gives an orientation to all further choices. The formation of this dominant inclination depends on our given situation—our body, our family, our background, our class, our country—all factors which we have not chosen but which contribute to organizing

[18] Mouroux, *op. cit.*, p. 155.

our human existence and to defining, to a certain degree, the ways we will act and the choices we will make.[19] That is why we can also speak of a liberty-in-engagement.

Man may establish his dominant inclination in either of the two directions to whose strivings he is subject. It may consolidate a "captive" liberty—that is, an increasing enslavement by our physical powers and appetites—or it may enhance what we have seen as "free," or real, liberty, the movement toward the harmonious integration of all our various activities in relation to the ultimate end of our being. This twofold possibility in the formation of the dominant inclination points to the importance of the first conscious choices.

Once the dominant inclination is established, our choices tend to revolve consistently around it; nevertheless we are not subject, as human beings, to determinism, and "captive" liberty need not persist forever. There are also, as we have noted, the *creating* acts of liberty, acts of conversion which involve a total break with the past or a decisively renewed assertion, by way of purification or of perversion, of the dominant inclination. These acts "constitute the most splendid proof of the abiding liberty of man."[20] They are always possible because the will, in that it is ordered to the infinite, cannot be limited by any of the many finite possibilities open to us in the form of various natural goods. They are, of course, difficult acts since they require us to step back and look at past choices, at positions dearly held, and to re-evaluate them, perhaps negatively. For this reason also they are rare. Nevertheless they are truly acts that mark the uniqueness and greatness of the human person.

[19] Cf. Emmanuel Mounier, *Be Not Afraid,* trans. Cynthia Rowland (London: Rockliff, 1951), p. 127.
[20] Mouroux, *op. cit.,* p. 158.

Thus we see the immense possibilities that liberty opens up for our realization as human persons both by means of the free acts which follow in the direction of a properly established dominant inclination, and by means of the creative acts in virtue of which we decide for, and seek to reach, the higher means of our perfection. Nevertheless, and insofar as we understand "freed" liberty to be not only our power of choosing indifferently but the growing harmonization and self-possession of our whole being, we have to acknowledge its connection with the activity that of its very nature tends to promote this harmonization. We refer to love. Freed liberty requires that our being shall be sustained by the force of a natural and supernatural love for the values and proper ends of man as they are ultimately personified in God. Love can thus be found intrinsically related to liberty to the extent that a proper love will of itself give form to our dominant inclination and will rightly direct all our free acts. This is the sense in which we are able to understand St. Augustine's counsel: *Dilige, et fac quod vis!* "Love, and do what you will!"

And we come now to speak formally of *love*.

Love is at its roots a movement of our appetitive forces seeking unity with an object seen as good.[21] We can conceive it in its metaphysical form, as the tendency we share with the universe as a whole to find union with the ultimate source of being, the good to which everything is oriented—God.

In our existence, love appears as a force of singular strength which defines all our activities, and which can be experienced in every one of our human ties. It is the psychological expression of the metaphysical tendency of our being, and as such, it manifests a deep craving for self-unification or self-integration, and for union with others and with God. The following

[21] Cf. St. Thomas, *Summa Theol.*, I–2.26,1.

analysis of St. Thomas' thought on love may serve to illustrate
this point:

Love is nothing but the exercise of our being, of our form of
being. . . . And since the fundamental activity of any being is to
realize the unity proper to it, all love must be an active tendency
toward unity, more or less intense, according to its degree of being. . . . In the degree of created spirits which is our own, this
activity prompts us to more and more intimate union, not only with
ourselves, but also with others and with God.[22]

Love is a force having reference to our being in itself and
our being with relation to others; in this sense it manifests
itself in two forms, or directions, which are united in the
same act of love. Martin D'Arcy speaks of them as self-regarding and other-centered love (the classic *Eros* and *Agape*).
He adds that both forms are necessary for the fulfillment of
our perfection. If our love were entirely open—that is, other-
centered—we might fear the loss of the integrity of our being.
Self-regarding love is the saving element of our personal
reality; it stands for reason and judgment, for truth "which
conforms to the essential nature of the self and the whole
order of being to which it belongs."[23] On the other hand, to
love just ourselves, or to love others exclusively out of self-
interest, means a denial of the very character of our being,
the metaphysical link with the creator. When we center exclusively on ourselves our love atrophies, it fails to become the
explicitation which finds genuine expression in the love of
others for their own sake.[24]

[22] Gilleman, *op. cit.*, p. 131.

[23] D'Arcy, *op. cit.*, p. 314.

[24] Psychologically explained, love includes the two movements of
which we are speaking as evident from this definition of "mature
love": "*union under the condition of preserving one's integrity,* one's
individuality." Erich Fromm, *The Art of Loving* (New York: Harper

Love as a tendency toward union appears at both the organic and rational levels of our being. Love proper is spiritual love, or the love that issues from the intellect and will and manifests itself in a genuine spiritual affectivity. However, this love is an activity of the whole human being, and therefore it is linked in some way with man's sensible being. It is expressed by means of our body, and it originates in some sensible experience which affects the intellect and will. Frequently, the physical forms of love are actually the source of properly human love. We may think, for example, of the instinctive love of a child for its mother, a love which in time may acquire the depth and maturity of the love of an Augustine for a Monica. Love thus becomes a purification—or more precisely, an elevation of the organic appetites to a plane whereon they are illumined by the rational powers, becoming spiritualized and capable of spiritualizing. It is evident that the more meaningful form of love must be that which incorporates sensible affectivity, including emotions and passions, since the unity of the person in the exercise of his defining activity can thus be assured. We shall refer later to the educational importance of this fact, but for the moment and as an illustration it is interesting to note the rising concern for a proper understanding of love in education, in terms not only of its spiritual component but also of its non-rational forms. Referring to the importance of non-rational love in religious

---

& Brothers, 1956), p. 20. Metaphysically, however, one can see how even our self-regarding love becomes other-centered by following the tendency of our being to unite with God. The love of the part for the whole is greater than the love of the part for itself, and since God is our whole, we love Him more than ourselves. In turn, this love of God unites both forms of love in their existential condition. "While preferring her own spiritual good above all other created persons, the soul can love the latter as children of God and not merely as reflections of her own self." Gilleman, *op. cit.*, p. 123.

education, Marc Oraison has declared that "the conditioning
of the higher level of the personality through the emotional
life, including the unconscious, is of such importance that a
system of education which does not take it into account must
inevitably result in the failure of its purpose."[25]

These reflections lead us to see in love a force which of its
very nature (its tendency to unite) is the integrative principle
of our being. It brings together our sensory activities and
affections and perfects them by incorporating them into the
activities of the intellect and will. We have already spoken of
its relation to liberty inasmuch as our decision to utilize the
proper means for attaining the good of our being depends on
the direction of our love. Love is also a result of liberty since
it does not really come into being in its human form until it
is accepted and welcomed.[26] And by accepting love we accept
the force that orders and harmonizes our being and elevates us
to the rank of free independent persons, capable of opening
ourselves to others and engaging with them in the reciprocal
communication of the richness of our selves.

Love is thus the power and activity which defines our
existence, since all our other activities find their part in it and
are integrated hierarchically by it. And the love which, illumined by the intellect and strengthened by the will, incorporates the innermost regions of our being, including our
organic life, is by far the strongest and most perfect form of
natural love.

Love and liberty in their relation to all our human activities
have helped us to see the means whereby man may reach his
perfection. However, this is only a natural perfection and is

[25] Marc Oraison, *Love or Constraint,* trans. Una Morrissy (New
York: P. J. Kenedy & Sons, 1959), p. 13.
[26] Mouroux, *op. cit.,* p. 204.

not a stable possession in our present condition. We know
that there is a still higher level to which man may aspire. It
will thus be our task to relate this natural perfection to two
of the most important virtues we have through the gift of the
supernatural life: faith and charity.

The believer is defined by *faith,* and faith is the virtue which
opens the way for the elevation and perfection of our whole
nature by grace. Hence it is important that we realize its
meaning. In its specific form, faith acts upon the intellect; it
is the gift which perfects our rational cognitive activities,
allowing us "to see" in obscurity the face of God and the
supernatural world. However, we must not conceive of faith as
simply connoting assent to a set of images, articles and concepts such as are contained in the Catholic creed.[27] Even
though faith has an irreducible intellectual content which
requires an intellectual assent, this assent is given through
mediation of its content to the person of God, and in this
sense it engages our whole being and not only our intellectual
faculties. We must see faith as the intimate adherence of the
intelligence, the will, and the heart to a living person.[28]

[27] Franz Arnold has asserted that ever since the Reformation, and
precisely because of the problems it posed, stress has been placed on
the intellectual assent in faith. As a consequence, speculative and
practical theology in the sixteenth and seventeenth centuries emphasized the content of faith and its integrity. This position, Arnold declares, has been dominant up to our own days with unfortunate consequences both for pastoral work and piety. Franz Arnold, "The Act of
Faith, A Personal Commitment," *Lumen Vitae,* V (April–September,
1950), 251–255.
[28] Cf. August Etcheverry, S.J., *Le Conflict Actuel des Humanismes*
(Paris: Presses Universitaires de France, 1955), p. 275. Cf. also, Jean
Mouroux, *I Believe, The Personal Structure of Faith,* trans. Michael
Turner (New York: Sheed and Ward, 1959). A major part of the
analysis of faith we are making is based on this little but excellent
work.

Faith has a twofold effect on man. First of all, a *personal* effect: it relates the human person to the person of God, establishing thereby the meeting of two persons. The obscurity of the act of faith is in the first place characteristic of the self-revelation of one person to another, which is always obscure to the reason; but it is intensified by the fact that here it is an infinite spirit revealing itself to a finite one. And the certitude of faith, whose firmness is not conceivable in terms of the purely intellectual evidence upon which it is based, must be ascribed to the assent we give to the word of a Person who knows. In the light of this, St. Thomas's assertion that in faith "it is the person to whose words the assent is given who is of principal importance" becomes meaningful.[29]

But faith also has a *personalizing* effect inasmuch as by uniting man to the personal God it raises him to his full dignity as a person. Faith *gives* a new dimension to freedom and inclines it toward the sphere of freed or supernaturalized liberty. It is a light, a principle of vision, which transforms the mind from within, giving a new orientation to human choices. It is an orientation toward beatitude in God—the defining good for a "freed" liberty. Faith also *rests* on liberty as it rests on the spiritual structure of the person. The object of faith, which is beatitude as offered to us by God in Christ, demands for its acceptance a personal commitment, renunciation and sacrifice insofar as it implies the way of the cross and an intellectual assent given without total understanding. In view of these factors, faith requires a choice, a positive decision which must be daily renewed. This decision rests naturally upon an act of liberty that prolongs our initial option, and above all on "creative" liberty:

[29] St. Thomas, *Summa Theol.*, 2.2.11,1.

The first act of faith is therefore, in the strict sense, an act of creative liberty, an act that changes a man and makes him *pass from death to life* (John V, 24), and makes him a son of God. The acts that follow carry on and strengthen the first and root it deeper; when the act of faith is renewed the choice and option is consolidated, they incline the spirit and master the flesh.[30]

However essential the virtue of faith is to the life of the Christian, an inquiry into its very roots and the force that ultimately keeps it alive has led theologians to dwell on the importance of charity. Faith, as we have seen, rests on the activities proper to the human person, the tendency toward truth and the exercise of freedom; but we have also seen how love, the movement of the rational appetite, acts as an integrative force in man's being, as the dynamic principle by which man becomes a person. In this sense it is possible to see the connection between faith as resting on a sound natural foundation in man and love elevated by grace to the perfection of charity. If faith rests upon nature, and if love is the force that promotes the integrity of this foundation, then love perfected by charity must be all the closer to faith and its perfection in human life. St. Thomas declares: "What perfection there is in faith is derived from charity, so that while charity possesses this perfection essentially, faith and the other virtues only participate in it."[31] Faith, which implies adherence to a Person who is not only truth but also happiness, cannot reach its object without the help of that activity which of its nature seeks happiness, love. And insofar as charity is the perfection of love, we can see how the attainment of the object of faith is possible only through charity.

Charity itself is the intrinsic elevation of our rational prin-

---

[30] Mouroux, *The Meaning of Man,* p. 183.
[31] St. Thomas, *De Veritate,* 14.5,3 and 4.

ciple of action, of love, inasmuch as it impels toward affective union.[32] But since love is born of, and takes in the whole of, man's dynamic forces, including those of his organic nature, we are able to see charity as the virtue which elevates the entire dynamism of our being, transforming our love into a divinized love. Charity is the principle by which God raises our natural being to a more perfect state of being, that of being in God. By giving Himself to us in charity God gives us of His being, makes us more fully ourselves, and allows us to come into an intimate union with Him. However, though charity is entirely God's gift to us, it does rest on our natural ability to love, on the acts in which we open ourselves to union. The air permeated by the light of the sun is the best image of our human love as it is penetrated by charity. This union of ours with God, and God's indwelling in us through charity, can be explained only by Christ, in whom the finite and infinite, the human and divine love, are perfectly united.

Thus charity is seen as the virtue that, by perfecting the integration of our natural powers, helps to bring our entire self into the supernatural order, making us more fully human, more fully persons. Properly it is the virtue which dynamically realizes in us the character we have received in virtue of God's creative activity—to be the image and likeness of the God who is love (I John 4:7).

In our analysis of the process of human perfecting in terms of liberty and love, and in terms of the supernatural gifts of faith and charity, we have dealt with what we might call the "vertical" integration of human existence. But this is an abstraction, for even though the perfection of our being requires the hierarchical ordination of our activities in terms of our

[32] Cf. Gilleman, *op. cit.,* p. 155.

end in God, this is never achieved without the other integration which we will call "horizontal." This is an integration of man as a being in relation with God as the source of this being.

We have already explained in what ways man is related to the universe, to nature, and to his fellow-men. The relation is one of dependence, for this natural context is a condition for self-realization. In other words, we need these relations for our physical and psychic existence; without them we are unable to raise ourselves to the full stature which is potentially ours as human beings. However, unless we somehow become aware of our own unique individuality in these relations and personalize them by infusing into them the activities proper to the human person, we shall merge with their objects, thus losing our identity.

We have also seen that the full meaning of the human person is found only when we transcend his natural existence and see him transformed by grace and in active communication with God. Hence we assert that ultimately the personalizing of man's relations is a divinizing or supernaturalizing of them by means of grace. More proximately, when we see that love is the activity which leads to the kind of union in which the integrity of the individual is not destroyed, and when we see charity-love as its perfection in the supernatural order, we conclude that love in its all-inclusive sense (natural and supernatural) is the force by which our relations cease to be a threat to our personal existence.

What does this entail concretely when we consider, for example, our relation to *nature?* (By nature we mean here the universe of beings both inanimate and animate which are located below the human level in the scale of existence.) First of all, we must learn to see nature not simply as an element

placed at our service for the satisfaction of needs. Our true
relation to nature demands that we recognize its significance,
that we personalize it by our superior faculties. This implies
that our powers of knowing are given us in order that we
may search without rest for the possibilities nature offers us,
and that we may incorporate its meanings within us. But inasmuch as our knowledge is perfected by faith, it means also
that we are to see in nature the Person who is hidden in it, the
God who while totally above nature, is nevertheless present in
His effects in every fibre of the earth, in every drop of water, in
every tool or instrument which helps to draw from virgin nature some meaningful good for human ends. Teilhard de
Chardin has pointed out that since the Incarnation, when the
Word actually assumed the material forms which also make
up the natural world, everything has become in a sense "Chris-
tified" and that consequently we find everywhere a real manifestation of the living God.[33] Our task as specified by St.
Thomas is to elevate nature to the higher degrees of being,[34]
to spiritualize it, as Teilhard would say, to use it as a steppingstone to God. Here we can find the ultimate greatness of our
activities, intellectual and physical, in their connection with
nature. In a special way, by seeing God in nature we are
compelled toward union, and here lies the importance of our
human power of love. The cosmic energy which gives cohesion
to every particle in the universe is similar in effect to love—
it is a cosmic love which impels nature to its end. Our union
or relation with nature is strengthened and spiritualized by our

[33] Cf. Pierre Teilhard de Chardin, *The Divine Milieu* (New York:
Harper & Brothers, 1960).

[34] "Those things which are nearest to the end [in this case man] are
more subject to the order whereby things are directed to the end, since
by their means even other things are ordered to the end." St. Thomas,
Contra Gentiles, 3.90.

free and personal love of God in nature, and of God as the
creator of nature. Thus it comes to add a new dimension to the
energy that keeps the universe in movement toward its end.

But to find God in nature, we must put ourselves into it,
we must find the place which is uniquely ours, and we must
love it as the mold in which our material and spiritual existence is rooted and nourished and through which we are
aided in finding a new facet of the reality of God.[35] The country in which we are born is nothing unless its men have a
genuine love for it as their mother earth. The same applies
to the more circumscribed environment constituted by the
home. All man's activities over nature to conquer it for human ends must be personalized if they are really to provide
him with more than a material gift. Somehow the capacity for
loving our work must be preserved even in the great industrial
centers, where the structure of labor tends rather to dehumanize man than to allow him to personalize his work. Ever wider
areas of nature can be conquered and personalized if man is
able to start with the feeling that there is a small area that has
received much of his love or that of those whom he has loved,
in which he has expressed himself as a person, and which because of this has led him to God. Then, as the poets see the
image of divine beauty in nature, man will find in his activities,
above all his work both manual and intellectual, and in the
possessions that nature gives him, the reflex of divine activity
and the presence of Christ, by whom all things are ever

[35] Walter J. Ong has pointed out repeatedly that though today there
is a deep-seated intellectual contact between the most remote places
and times, we are fatally lacking in any increase in our felt internal
experience of nature. Cf. W. J. Ong, S.J., "Microcosm and Macrocosm:
Religion, Scholarship, and the Resituation of Man," Paper prepared
for the Frank L. Weil Institute for Studies in Religion and the Humanities, Cincinnati, Ohio, January 17–19, 1961, p. 14. (Mimeographed.)

"created, sanctified, endowed with life, blessed and bestowed upon us," and through whom, in the Holy Spirit, the universe will be led to the Father.

It is now time to turn to what is probably the most important of man's natural ties: the tie to his *fellow-men*. The increasing movement of socialization to which we referred at the beginning of this chapter, and the problem of the mass society and culture, make vitally significant the correct understanding of the links between men and their present-day importance for the development of the individual. Hence we shall briefly refer to man's capacity for entering into personal relationships and for giving rise to community life.

In our study of the human person we have seen that a fundamental trait of his is the ability to "open" to others, somehow to effect a joining of his own self with that of another. This capacity, which is properly the result of the human activity of loving, terminates in what is called personal communion and is the basis of the type of association which we call "community." As such, this form infuses the wider realm of associated activities which we call "society" with a deeper meaning, the meaning of association at the human, personal level. Without the penetration of society by the spirit of community, society becomes simply a servant to the needs of men in their material-biological reality, or an entity arbitrarily superimposed on the individual's reality.

Community, as we have stated, is born of the capacity of the human person to open himself to others, to communicate the overflowing riches of his being, and thereby to unite himself by internalized bonds to the society of men on which he depends for his existence. Human communities are an expression of relations between persons which are interiorized through love (resting, of course, on knowledge). As such they retain the traits which genuine love offers: the integrity of each

person and the communion of all. They entail the predominance of the psychological qualities of personal love: care,
defined by Fromm as the active concern for the life and the
growth of that which we love;[36] responsibility—a readiness to
respond to the other, to his needs; respect—the ability to see
the other in the uniqueness of his own reality, to understand
him not as an object and a means but as a being with an existence and task of his own. Such an ability depends on the
knowledge of the other's uniqueness. Personal relations entail
as a whole, a mutual spiritual integration of one *in* the other,
a mutual spiritual complementation of one *by* the other, and a
mutual responsibility of one *for* the other.

Man cannot develop without coming into relations with
others; but just as it is inscribed in his nature to associate, it
is also inscribed that he become an individual, a unique
reality. To reconcile these two demands of his being, the appeal to a communication transcending the physico-biological
relations of society is necessary, and this is the appeal to
communities based on personal relationships, which adds a
new dimension to social life.

The realization of ourselves as human persons is intimately
bound up with the situation of community life—and it is this
fact that leads us to acknowledge the possibilities inherent in
the current trend toward collectivization. Teilhard de Chardin
asserts that to be fully ourselves we must move in the direction of convergence: "The goal of ourselves, the acme of our
originality, is not our individuality but our person; and according to the evolutionary structure of the world, we can
only find our person by uniting together."[37] But he adds that
it will not suffice for us just to join up together anyhow, we
must do it by a contact of center to center, a contact which is

[36] Fromm, *The Art of Loving*, p. 26.
[37] Teilhard de Chardin, *The Phenomenon of Man*, p. 263.

essentially achieved by love. When we observe the degrading effects on the individual of today's collectivization, which are quite contrary to its possibilities, we realize that the contact established between the members of society is still superficial and lacking in personal love.

The possibility, however, of developing a form of community able to give meaning and life to the movement of collectivization and personal identity to man, is given only if we recognize a source and a point of convergence for the human community as a whole which stands above it. By recognizing that the unique reality of the human person depends for its existence on God, we also see that the community as an association of persons likewise owes its integrity to Him. And if we acknowledge that man ultimately achieves the fullness of his personal reality in communion with God through grace, then we must also see the meaning of the community as found ultimately in reference to the supernatural order. Concretely, if we acknowledge that the human person attains his highest reality when his activities of loving are transformed and perfected in charity, so also we must say that authentic community is, in the last analysis, a living relation of charity, and that in this sense it participates in the love between the persons of the Trinity. The mystery of the community of Three Persons in the Godhead is the model and guarantee of all human communities. This mystery, by revealing the community of love which exists between three distinct Persons, each of whom totally possesses the Divine Nature, teaches us that there is no inherent opposition between person and community, but that on the contrary, community can only be conceived as a community of persons by charity-love.

The possibility of a growth of mankind into one all-embracing community marked by love and converging with the whole universe in God (as Teilhard has suggested) can be envisioned ultimately because we are a redeemed race, because we are able to call ourselves children of the Father. Henri de Lubac, who has studied the abiding social significance of Catholicism, points out that even in the solitary life of the mystic there is never absent a consciousness of the unity of mankind and of a communion of love in the Father.[38]

Communion in charity is vitally exemplified in the Mystical Body, the union of all in Christ which leads into that perfect community which is the Blessed Trinity. In the Mystical Body we become all one in Christ (Gal. 3:28) and are united in Him to the Father and the Holy Spirit. But also through our incorporation in the Mystical Body we remain, like each person in the Trinity, unique persons—each one of us a true child of God.

Hence our perfection as persons goes hand in hand with our relations to our fellow-men as they are sustained by a natural love perfected through charity. Ultimately we must say that without society—or, more specifically, without human communities and the greater community which issues from our union with Christ—we cannot reach the reality to which the Father has called us: to be fully personal selves. This seems to be the real meaning of the "new man" in whom we are to be renewed. In this respect, de Lubac has asserted that in the Church's tradition the meaning of the "new man" is not separated from the notion of the Church, of the Body of Christ. He points out that there has not been sufficient attention paid to the fact that in the Epistle to the Colossians mention of the "new man" is coupled with reference to the unique Image, the

[38] Henri de Lubac, S.J., *Catholicism: A Study of Dogma in Relation to the Corporate Destiny of Mankind* (New York: Sheed and Ward, 1958), p. 190.

image of Him that created him, and to "Christ . . . all, in all."[39]

Our preceding discussion has helped us to see in what way the movement toward personal realization, which is a moral imperative for man, is a movement of integration. It consists in the perfecting and elevating of the non-rational forces in man through the proper rational activities of knowledge and love, and the exercise of liberty in its dimensions of choice and action. It is further an incorporation of man's rational nature into the realm of grace, especially by the virtues of faith and charity—these resting on, and sustained by, liberty. An excursion into the depths of this process presents the unifying force of love in all its dimensions as its essential dynamism. The culmination of love in charity enables us to see that, in the last analysis, this task of integration is a work of grace by which man participates in the God who created him and sustains his being as that of a unique person.

But the movement of integration is also viewed horizontally, as a movement by which man extends to the entire realm of his relations with nature and society the activities which define him as a person, and particularly charity-love. In this sense, man's natural dependence upon the objects of his relations can be interiorized and integrated into his movement toward God. We may now add, in an effort to clarify the meaning of this process, that in virtue of the power of secondary causality which God has conferred on all his creatures—the universe and mankind—everything which is, is able to lead to God.[40] If we transfer this philosophical principle to the existential plane—that is, to the level of human development in the world—we are able to conceive how a deep relationship to creatures—nature and, above all, men and human ideas—in

[39] *Ibid.*, p. 120.
[40] St. Thomas, *Summa Theol.*, 6.1,1.

terms of the bond of a natural love supernaturalized by charity, and a knowledge illuminated by faith, can lead us to God and the fulfillment of our being. It is of the utmost importance to understand this, since we do depend on these relations in virtue of our existence in time and space, and hence to conceive their objects as so many mediating elements which partake in the Mediator's role is always a true possibility open to us for communion with God. This possibility is seen in a special manner in the community. It is through our relations with men that we can truly love, for love at bottom is only possible between persons (that is, as a reciprocal communication in virtue of the rational activities of the intellect and will). And this love, because it is a love between creatures who are directly made in the image and likeness of God and redeemed by Christ, is no doubt a powerful means for our union with God, as well as for our personal realization. Real natural love for men, including the sensible elements which are ordered by the rational powers, needs to be crowned by charity; but charity at the same time rests on natural love as its foundation. The formation of communities sustained by charity-love has thus the double function of giving new life to society and a concrete realization to the Mystical Body of Christ; of making the Church not only an institution but a living community of love in Christ. Men thus become, in a special way, mediators (because incorporated in Christ), and human love illumined by charity becomes one of the most powerful steppingstones to an understanding of the love of God and to unity with Him. Theologically, Gilleman asserts, love illumined by charity is a mediation, and "a mediation is never a means that can be left aside once it has been used to attain the end. It is the intermediary, the actual 'visibility,' ever necessary to attain God through the community of men."[41]

41 Gilleman, *op. cit.*, p. 298.

THE TEMPORAL MISSION OF MAN

Our analysis of the human vocation as a process of integration cannot be completed unless we see this process as taking place in the specific temporal context in which man is situated and under the existential conditions that it poses. Insofar as the human person is an incarnate reality inserted in the universe, he not only depends upon the conditions that this insertion poses but is also challenged by these conditions to a specific activity to be performed with regard to them. Secondary causality belongs to man as to every other creature, but it belongs in a special way to him as a being endowed with freedom. In this sense, each individual by his actions participates in the activity of God Himself as He manifests His power and care over the world at every historical moment. Hence the person becomes not only a vocation toward self-realization, but a vocation toward self-realization as an instrument of God in his own time.

We may speak of a threefold vocation or mission or task of man: a general mission, a personal one, and a time-conditioned mission which brings the preceding two into the given temporal framework.

The *general* mission is the task leading to the fulfillment of man's reality as a person and as a child of God, and of his reality and responsibility as a member of the Body of Christ; it depends as a whole on the order of creation and on God's general providence. Ultimately it is expressed in the Christian call to be perfect like the Father.

The *personal* mission is the individualized and unique form that the general mission takes for every man, one which rests on his natural potentialities and the special graces given to him—all manifestations of the *idea exemplaris* of the individual which has pre-existed in the divine mind from all eternity. Though individual, this mission has nevertheless a social dimension which must always be considered. It is personal precisely because it involves a task which the human community needs, and more concretely, one which the Body of Christ and its visible manifestation, the Church, needs; a task which only the individual can perform but which is discovered and is realized in the community. In this sense, one can say that everybody is called to sanctity but that each individual receives his own special call, his charisma, along with a special task to realize. The following words which were written as an introduction to a study of the mission of St. Thérèse of Lisieux may serve to illustrate what we are saying:

The mission which each individual receives contains within itself the form of sanctity which has been granted to him and is required of him. In following that mission he fulfills his appropriate capacity for sanctity. This sanctity is essentially social, something outside the arbitrary disposition of any individual. For each Christian God has an Idea which fixes his place within the membership of the Church; this Idea is unique and personal, embodying for each his appropriate sanctity. There is no danger that it will not prove high enough or broad enough in any instance. Indeed, it is so sublime, so intimately bound to divine infinity, that it is perfectly achieved by no-one except Mary. The Christian's supreme aim is to transform his life into this Idea of himself secreted in God, this "individual law" freely promulgated for him by the pure grace of God.[42]

The *time-conditioned* or temporal mission can be seen as the form which the general vocation of man takes in a specific epoch, being thus the immediate framework for the discovery of the personal vocation. Naturally, this mission is intrinsically related to the conditions of the times, particularly its prob-

---

[42] Hans Urs von Balthasar, *Thérèse of Lisieux*, trans. Donald Nicholl (New York: Sheed and Ward, 1954), pp. xii–xiii.

lems and needs. Our discussions in the previous chapters have referred us to one of the important problems which confront us today: the condition of man and of the community. In what we have developed thus far in this chapter, we have endeavored to touch upon the meaning of man in those aspects which have reference to these problems; and this leads us to at least one of the elements in the time-conditioned mission or task of modern man.

Man has appeared before us as a person of unique dignity because of his nature and because of his vocation, a vocation to self-realization by way of an interrelated vertical and horizontal integration. In this light, we are able to see that at the source of the modern situation lies the inability of man to carry out this integration. A number of developments have contributed to this, as have also mutilated theories of man in the moment of their practical application. Modern man, as we have seen, tends to be deprived of his sense of oneness with nature (in spite of the fact that nature is constantly providing more possibilities for the satisfaction of his physical and spiritual needs); this is the result, in part, of the type of work he must perform, the lack of a direct contact with nature, and the lack, in large sectors of the world's population, of the bare necessities of human life. Modern man, we have frequently stated, tends to be unable to communicate in terms of an intimate opening of the self to the other, and of authentic self-giving; and this in spite of the increase in means of external communication. To a large extent, modern man is unable to find the small communities, such as the family, capable of ministering not only materially but also spiritually to his needs as a social being. And suffering from this isolation, man tends to fail in the elaboration of a world of personal reflections about reality, and in the acknowledgment and commitment to

supra-temporal values and ideals which, as a being characterized by reason, he needs for his realization. We complain of a
lack of critical thinking, of the emptiness of mind in so many
individuals who are attuned only to the succession of images
and impressions of the moment. These are manifestations of
the lack of a communitarian atmosphere in which personal
communication and affective security can contribute to directing the mind's attention to its proper objects and helping it
toward the exercise of its proper activities. This situation
further impairs the will and the free acts which depend on it.
Lack of clarity in thought diminishes the possibility of the
decisions and actions which are needed to preserve human
values. And without the proper exercise of these activities
man falls victim first to conformity, then to the mass, and
finally, to the all-absorbing collective.

In this situation the supernatural orientation which should
come to crown the individual's existence is impaired. Without
experiences, at the natural level, of personal communication,
of authentic love, it is difficult (though not necessarily im-
possible, since grace exceeds all our natural potentialities) to
understand the love of God.[43] Likewise, without an experience
of what it means to commit ourselves personally and responsi-
bly for what we believe or hold to be true in any of our spheres
of activity, it is hard to maintain a lived fidelity to our Chris-

[43] Delcuve voices a widespread opinion among those who connect
the findings of psychology with the quality of religious experience. He
says: "If so many children remain today indifferent to the paternity of
God, to the generous intimacy of the divine persons, to the beauty of
the great Christian family, is it not in part due to the fact that they
have not known a true fatherly love, a united home? . . . They are
lacking that natural experience which in virtue of a 'psychological
analogy' might communicate a real and vivid current to a religious
teaching." Georges Delcuve, S.J., "Le Problème de la formation re-
ligieuse dans le monde moderne," *Lumen Vitae*, IV (April–June), 214.

tian beliefs. Or, if we have never experienced the warmth and security of a home, it will be difficult even to long for a heavenly home in the heart of the Father.

The above statements point out a possible cause (and we believe it is an essential cause) of the main problem we have to contend with today: the unbelief of our times which turns culture away from the very source of its humanness. It is the unbelief either of the "absolute" or of the "practical" atheist; of the man who totally renounces his dependence on God and denies his existence, and of the man who, while giving lip service to God, fashions his life no differently from the absolute atheist.[44] The far-reaching task of our times, the ultimate time-conditioned mission, is to combat what Pope John XXIII has termed in his encylical *Mater et Magistra* "the most perniciously typical aspect of the modern era":

the absurd attempt to reconstruct a solid and fruitful temporal order prescinding from God, the only foundation on which it can endure, and to want to celebrate the greatness of man by drying up the font from which that greatness springs and from which it is nourished, hence restraining and if possible extinguishing man's sighing for God.

This is the phenomenon of secularization of which philosophical naturalism is the theory; and which, as we have seen from our study of Marx and Dewey, even though offering

[44] Jean Lacroix has suggested that absolute atheism (which is a modern development) has had the value of laying bare the insufficiency of a purely theoretical belief in God lacking in practical commitment. "The Meaning and Value of Atheism Today," *Cross Currents* (Summer, 1955), 203–219. In the same tone, Maritain has declared that absolute atheism "is in first place the fruit and the condemnation of practical atheism, and its image reflects in the mirror of divine wrath." *La Signification de l'athéisme contemporain* (Paris: Desclée de Brouwer, 1949), p. 41.

valuable insights, suffers from grave limitations which justify the Pope's assertions.

The over-all task for the Christian is thus to help to bring God back to our culture. It is an obligation given voice everywhere in Christian circles. However, it is not always so clear (especially with respect to educational applications) that this task cannot be accomplished simply by appealing for an increase in religious life, frequently understood as an increase of participation in religious organizations; that somehow we have to begin by strengthening the individual's personality so he may be capable of the firm decisions that the conflicting currents in a mass and secularized society make imperative. Strong and responsible Christians must be fully present in every field of activity, both of the intellectual and practical order, so as to offer their contribution to progress in our knowledge and conquest of the world, discovering by this means ever new phases of "Christ all in everything."[45]

The above reflections serve to complete our previous discussions. We stressed the need for awareness of the situation we have been analyzing throughout, and now we add that this awareness must lead to action; that consequently we must seek to *form* the type of man who will meet the crisis, and we must help to make man, in particular the Christian, aware of his time-conditioned mission, which is precisely to meet this crisis.

In conclusion, may we summarize the meaning of this mission or task of the Christian in our century, which, by resting on the general mission, will give meaning to the very special task each one has to perform in the community of the Church. We start by acknowledging that our times evidence a growing

[45] Cf. August Brunner, S.J., "Christentum heute," *Stimmen der Zeit*, CLIII (1953), 35–46.

movement toward a "coming together" of mankind (a movement rooted in human nature itself which has in all times been
the basis for the existence of societies, as it is for the modern
developments which have made possible a growing external
communication). We also note the rapid changes which are
removing the elements of stability and rootedness upon which
man has been able to count until now for his realization. And
we acknowledge that this last factor makes for the dangerous
aspect in the *present* collectivization trends: a deviation in the
direction of a mass society. A recognition of the "deformed"
situation of man and society, as well as an awareness of the
importance—and genuine possibilities—of this irreversible
"coming together" of mankind, gives expression, then, to the
present task. It rests on the formation of a "new community,"
or rather, of a new universal communitarian spirit which
receives its meaning from actual small spheres of community
life wherein the forces of love act as the unifying and stabiliz-
ing bond, enabling these communities to become centers of
human life which radiate out into the world, with which they
will never lose contact. Such communities, we think, may
contribute to restoring the integrity of the human ties. But to
be true centers of community life they will have to be constituted by persons—that is, by individuals who are not only
relatively free of the maladies arising from the lack of roots
and the tendencies toward passive conformity but are also
vitally aware of their responsibilities and capable of critical
thought, decisive action and fidelity to principles which does
not depend upon a great number of rules and prescriptions.

These are the "new men" who will give meaning to the "new
communities" which we see as of vital necessity in the modern
world, whose formation we see as the time-conditioned task

of our century, and particularly of the Christian in our century. To form these new men and new communities is, to a great extent, the dynamic aspect of the *ordo essendi* (the objective reality) which defines educational endeavors.

4

EDUCATING
THE "NEW MAN" FOR
THE "NEW COMMUNITY"

OUR PROBLEM in this chapter is a moral problem which re-
solves itself into a religious question: How shall we succeed
educationally in forming a type of man able to cope with the
current mass trends?, and how will Catholic education succeed
in forming a convinced Christian who works for a renewed
Christian world? These two questions are related, and the
answer to the second depends to a large extent upon the
answer to the first.

We will try to deal with these questions not so much in
terms of a "cure-all" remedy as of a general orientation. This
will have the object of opening our eyes to things we probably
already know, to means we probably already have, but which
we have perhaps not yet related creatively and synthetically
to the modern problems in society.

There are two elements which we are especially taking into
account. One is the immense impact of social forces upon
modern man. It is this that makes us concentrate upon approaches which we believe to be necessary in such educational
communities as the school and the family—social institutions
of primary importance for human development. The second

element is implicit in the first. It suggests that we cannot have our ideal educational communities unless we strive in a special way to work with existing elite groups and individuals (by the elite we mean those which are less marked than the average by the depersonalizing traits and mass trends of society). We believe that if they are prepared to assume the special responsibility of helping to renew society, we may hope for healthy educating communities forming healthy men. Hence, everything that will be said has the implicit aim of awakening among elite groups potential educators and potential parents to a great task; it has, from the point of view of Catholic activities, implicit suggestions for the education of the laity as Christian apostles in our times.

Because of the broad nature of our objectives we shall be forced to leave aside some issues which normally belong to a treatment of educational problems. Hence we shall not give specific consideration to the curriculum best ordered to the formation of a new man and of a new community, nor the type of school system, organization or administration suitable for this purpose, although we may make some incidental references to these aspects to the extent that our material calls for them. We shall concentrate on the *mode* (a somewhat abstract way of expressing a blending of attitudes, approaches, and means) best suited for achieving the natural-supernatural integration of man—the fully developed person and the completely formed Christian person, and the new communitarian spirit for our times. And for this purpose we shall artificially separate education for the natural from education for the supernatural integration of man.

A word about the orientation of this chapter: it is in its fundamentals borrowed from the educational principles and practices of a contemporary movement of Catholic action, the

Schoenstatt Apostolic Movement.[1] We have chosen this orientation (the influence is stronger in the second part of this chapter) because of its special concern, ever since its origins, with the problems we have been considering all along.[2] The movement in question has attempted, both in the education of its members and in the education it gives through its members, to help improve the modern mass condition of society insofar as it poses a moral and religious problem. Whatever we draw from its principles[3] we shall endeavor to relate to the view of

[1] This movement, having as its object to contribute to the moral-religious renewal of the world in Christ through Mary, was founded the 18th of October, 1914, in Schoenstatt, Germany, by Father Joseph Kentenich, S.A.C. It is organized in a branch of lay apostolate (families, men, women, youth and children) and leading Secular Institutes. The most important and numerous of these institutes is the Institute of Schoenstatt Sisters of Mary working in Europe, Africa, Australia, North and South America.

[2] In the program preceding the foundation of the Movement, Fr. Kentenich, foreseeing consequences of importance in the rising trends of society, told the group of young boys who were to become the founding generation: "We must learn, under the protection of Mary, to educate ourselves as free, firm, and priestly characters." This program has remained basic to all subsequent educational activities of the Schoenstatt Movement.

[3] The educational activities of Schoenstatt rest on a principle common to all true forms of education: the sound harmony between theory and life. Practically this means that we do not forget life in order to conform to theory, nor do we reject theory in favor of life. From the angle of theory, these educational activities rest upon a Thomistic view of the universe and of man, particularly secondary causality and the principle of harmonious unity between nature and grace. On the side of life, the practice and experiences afforded by the development of the Movement have led its founder to realize the value of findings in clinical and experimental psychology insofar as they have revealed the importance of irrational factors and unconscious motivation in human life; and inasmuch as they have provided knowledge of elements in human behavior which can be conveniently utilized for educational purposes. Likewise, there is recognition of the value of studies of the dynamics of group action and their impact upon human development. We thus refer the readers to works in social psy-

man presented in the previous chapter; and with the help of some other contributions from contemporary Catholic thought we shall attempt a synthesis. We hope that such a synthesis will serve at least as a starting-point for further reflections and practical experiences concerning the problems here discussed.

EDUCATION AND NATURAL INTEGRATION

Basic to the education of the whole personality, to the healthful expression of the non-rational forces in human life and their incorporation into the higher human activities, is the condition of the individual's relations to the external world. Education of the personality must be achieved within the context of a sound and normal dependence on this external world; it is a dependence which, more than merely physical, implies a habitual, felt experience of contact and security involving both rational and organic activities. We know that because of the many conflicting factors in modern society, man's conscious bonds with objects in the external world have been weakened. Hence the need for attention to those means whereby man may once again develop healthy natural roots or ties (education in the family), and the means also by which these roots may be reinforced (education in school and other institutions of society). To cure the sickness of modern man we must cure its source. Then, and only then, will the education of the individual in his ability to reflect, to decide freely, and especially to love, have any meaning.

---

chology and psychology such as those of C. G. Jung, Erich Fromm, Carl Rogers, Karen Horney, Karl Stern and others. The work of the Gestalt psychologists is also of value in their stress upon the unitary and wholistic character of human nature and development. These works may serve to deepen the understanding of the problems we deal with and of the educational orientation we propose to offer.

The need for roots in human existence is, as we have seen, directed toward two natural objects: society and the material world. The link with society becomes a felt experience for the individual (a satisfaction of his social need) only by means of roots in *personal relationships* and in a *world of ideas and values* mediated by such relationships. The link with nature becomes a felt experience when it is symbolized for the individual in a *home* (including his country, home town, house and all the objects for his subsistence and well-being, and in the work performed there). The task of education is, then, to develop and deepen this threefold set of personally experienced roots conceived as organically interrelated,[4] and to form, on this basis, a self-possessed personality. Such a task is accomplished by keeping in mind the fundamental human powers of knowledge and reflection, love, and freedom.

We shall thus deal with the above elements in terms of the traditional educational factors: the educational process from the angle of the educator-educand relationships; and the educational process from the angle of two educational societies, the family and school. These two aspects are, of course, only theoretically disjoined.

The Educator-Educand Relationship. Inability to communicate and to love—a terrible individual loneliness—marks one of the phases of contemporary society. The effectiveness in turning this "inability" into a positive "ability" determines

[4] The original German expression that the Schoenstatt educational theory adopted to explain this network of natural roots is *Natuerliche Bindungsorganism,* an organism of natural bonds. When German existentialists refer to the uprooted condition of modern man they often speak of a dissolution of *Bindungen,* having in mind the sort of *felt* relationship which integrates the emotional and intellectual life with the objects of natural relationships. As we shall see later, the *natuerliche Bindungsorganism* is completed by an *uebernatuerliches Bindungsorganism,* a supernatural organism of bonds.

the value of personal contacts between educator and educand. This contact as a lively interchange between persons has always been crucial to education. Today it is ever more so.

Personal bonds between the educator and the educand promote, on the part of the latter, a growth from relatively non-rational and emotional forms of love and attachment to forms which, controlled by reason, yield self-independence and a sense of spiritual union. In this development the initial stages are not progressively suppressed but progressively ordered. The educator offers his genuine love, encouraging and awakening the first instinctive forms of affection in a child. The child *feels* and *knows* the love that is given to him. And the educator can and must orient the relationship toward its gradual spiritualization and transformation.

The educator, of course, must himself be able to love rightly, to give his affection without either losing his individuality or egoistically seeking the satisfaction of some unfulfilled need. In other words, he has overcome or is at least relatively free of what psychologists term narcissistic tendencies (tendencies to see as real only what exists in himself, and to experience and treat everything else from the point of view of his own well-being). He frees himself from such tendencies by cultivating the spirit of objectivity—the power to recognize his own limitations—and the power of projecting himself creatively in the external world.

The educator makes his an other-centered orientation which keeps in mind the unique individuality of the educand. He loves his child or student not because of what the child or student does to please him or imitate him. He loves because he wants to awaken and develop the resources hidden in the child's being. He thus respects the educand for what he is, and furthermore, never wavers in his confidence. Confidence

is most vital to him, for he knows that love grows and is
nourished by it. He has confidence because he believes in the
goodness of human nature despite its limitations. He believes
in the common capacity to know, to love, and to act freely;
he believes in the common potentiality for integration and
harmony in the human powers. He knows that confidence does
not precede love but is rather a manifestation of love; he knows
that where there is genuine love there is also genuine faith
and trust in the loved one; and he knows that the careful
cultivation of this faith increases love.

Frequently as an educator he is disappointed in his endeavors; an action completely unexpected and contrary to his
desires, to the rules of order and even morality, tends to
weaken his trust. Yet he realizes that if he is to be a true
educator, especially today, he must hold on to his attitude of
confidence. He knows he must not allow disappointment to
injure his love. He does not, however, close his eyes to faults
and irresponsibility; on the contrary, he tries to arouse the
"sinner" to repentance and tries to develop in the child a fine
perception of what right action is. He does this by trying to
place him in an environment where he can experience right
living and habituate himself to it. He also does it by exhorta-
tion and, when necessary but less frequently, by punishment.
He knows, however, that the quality of punishment rests on
the age of the offender and the degree of the offense, and that
it should always be motivated by love. With repentance he
gives new energy to his love. Moral education entails the
increasing realization on the part of the educand that faults
are essentially a breach in love, and that to recognize and
admit them means to restore and increase the stream of love.

What are the *effects* of this educational relationship? In the
first place, as shown, the educand's non-rational and emotional

forces are awakened and given an ordered object of expression. Educationally speaking, these forces are utilized as means for bringing the educand into a living contact with the objective world the educator wishes to present to him. We shall see later how a mother, for example, helps a child to extend his attachment for her to include other people.

Secondly, personal relationships awaken the growing powers of thought and of liberty. The first search for truth is a search for that which is in the person loved. In terms of education this means that the educator strives incessantly to embody truth in himself, however conscious he may be of his own errors and limitations. Oraison says in this regard, when talking about the father:

It is essential that he should make them understand very early that like themselves he, too, is capable of making mistakes; and that he, too, is engaged in the endless search for perfection. It is essential that he should know enough to apologize formally to his children, even when they are very young, for faults he has committed or mistakes he has unwittingly made. His children's confidence in him will be multiplied because of it: "You can tell Daddy anything because he is honest and he knows when he has been wrong."[5]

In the personal bond the educator establishes between himself and the pupil he has a powerful tool for guiding the individual in the development of his reflective power. When the child's understanding has gradually begun to develop, the educator takes care that things are no longer presented baldly, as arbitrary commands. He knows that no punishment, no demand, is effective if the child who is capable of knowing "why" is not allowed to do so. By encouraging reflection and

[5] Oraison, *op. cit.,* p. 135.

understanding the educator directs the mind of the educand to an increasing number of objects and situations existing outside the immediate realm of personal contacts. Truth is discovered in others, in books, in living experiences.

The awakening of the desire for truth brings with it a simultaneous tendency to evaluate. Personal relationships introduce the educand into the world of values, beliefs, attitudes held by the educator. The growing child clings at first unconsciously to this world, which we will call "ideological" and which colors much of his early evaluation. As his capacity to reflect increases, the educator directs it toward understanding the objectivity of the ideological world; he helps the child establish points of comparison between this world and new experiences. He hopes that thereby the educand will acquire a personal conviction of what is true and objective in the world of ideas he has made unconsciously his own. He knows that there will be elements which will not stand the test of truth or that the individual will view from a different angle; hence he realizes that his own world of ideas and values and that of the child will be partially different. He knows this result is sound and is the real goal of personality education. However, if he acknowledges a basic ideological structure resulting from the common elements in human nature and reality (natural law), he recognizes also that the goal of education is *not* to have every individual erect an *arbitrary* personal world of values. That it is rather to help him achieve a rational (and at the same time affective) acceptance of that which objectively conforms to natural law and stands the test of truth, an acceptance which is personal and free. He knows also that it entails, in the erection of a value world, a personal *search* for truth. A child may grow up in a home in which there is a fundamental recognition of natural law and a set of beliefs and

values which conform to it; the child's education will then be
mostly one of a progressive understanding of this world and
a progressive incorporation of it, giving him a framework
from which to deal with all new situations about which he
knows nothing. But the child who grows up without this experience—the experience of an objective and stable ideological
starting-point—will have nothing to sustain his power of
thought and reflection, and his actions, save the pressure of
circumstances from moment to moment. He thus needs to
experience elsewhere what has been denied him, and he will
need an extremely strong education for reflection.

Thought is intimately connected with action. Even though
man acts to a great extent as a subject of habit, these habits
result initially from reflection or, if not, they are sustained at
one point or another by conscious awareness. On the strength
of personal relations and of experientially acquired values and
beliefs, the individual is guided not only to deal reflectively
with important situations but somehow to assert his position
regarding these situations; he is to make decisions and to carry
them out, bearing responsibility for the outcomes. In an
atmosphere of love and security, decisions are demanded from
individuals; in other words, there is an education for freedom.
When the educator personally exemplifies a strong capacity
for reflection and decision; when he helps the maturing individual to develop the same pattern before certain situations;
when he provides opportunities for these situations to come
up (gives, within the limits of the individual's subjection to
order and authority, many possibilities for free action), he
is educating for freedom. The educator, recognizing the sense
in which freedom applies to decisions which prolong previous
options, is careful to correct decisions and attitudes early on.
He also gives opportunity for the individual to make decisions

for which he is not prepared, thus furthering the "creative" meaning of liberty. In educating for freedom he is aware that he must work progressively from external controls to inner controls of behavior, and that only when there is a predominance of the latter is there a real ground for freedom.

The active interchange between educator and educand leads into contact with nature. The personalizing influence of the educator on the world around him makes it a vital source of felt security for the educand. We find this, for example, in the father who walks around the garden or the nearby park with his son, telling him about the different birds and plants, or who in the night points to the stars and the moon and shows how these things are connected with his child's life. Man needs to feel that he is not an isolated unit in a hostile universe, that he is a part, truly a microcosm, a being who stands above but who is also protected by the universe.

Creativity is finally the most powerful fruit of personal contacts and of the felt contacts with a world of ideas and nature that personal relationships insure. Creativity brings the individual out of himself and into the external world, and does so in virtue of the unique development of human powers which prevents absorption in this external world. It makes the individual work for others, discover, reflect on the deep meaning of things, act in an effort to transform nature physically, and strive to reach the world of good and beauty in nature and make it present symbolically. Creativity, however, also keeps the individual an integral reality. Not everybody can be creative in the same way; but in one form or another it is always a genuine human expression, essential to education, that living personal contacts help to develop.

As a whole, we may say that a personal contact between educator and educand is the most important vehicle by which an individual is introduced into felt contacts with other persons, ideas and nature, and it is this entire set of effects that determines the educational value of such relationships. However, this value normally is not given in a vacuum. It relies for the most part on the existence of social institutions. In these institutions we find the conditions for human personality to flourish, and to flourish by being sustained in an atmosphere of rootedness which above all is made up of their communitarian spirit. Let us then relate all we have said about the educator-educand relationship to the family and the school.

The Family. The need for roots (which involves the individual's non-rational tendencies and his rational activities) finds its first and most important form of satisfaction in the family. We speak of it as "first" in a chronological sense, but we also consider it most "important," because the family provides as a whole the three objects of the human need for rootedness: persons, ideas and values, and a home. It is also most important because, as clinical psychology has disclosed, the matter of adequate or inadequate satisfaction in early life of human needs has consequences that mark much of an individual's later life. Thus the person who has been unable to attach himself affectively to any other for a long period of his early life will find it difficult later on to love and communicate humanly. The same is true of the individual who has never experienced early opportunities to decide freely but has always been "obliged" or "decided for"; he will have great difficulty in coping with a mass society. Hence the contemporary educational importance of the family!

At the core of the family's educational endeavors lies an extending and orienting of the original contacts which a child experiences, leading to an increased independence in thought and existence.

How do we understand the *extending* function? A child at birth depends in almost every way upon his mother; she embodies for him all that is real and secure. Mother not only nourishes the child physically but responds also to his emotional needs. She is linked affectively to him. As he grows, however, his mother helps him widen his horizon and establish new contacts. Through her the child becomes aware of his father and of his brothers and sisters. These persons in turn help the mother extend the original relationship by their interest in and closeness to the child. Daddy helps occasionally with feeding, an older sister learns how to hold the child when Mother is busy, and the little brother plays with him, arousing his joy and laughter. The child begin to extend his feelings to these persons. Simultaneously, as his senses develop, he also becomes aware of objects in his room, in the house, which have "something" of the persons he already knows. The discovery of the external world may bring a crisis—the feeling of isolation; however, it is overcome when the family helps him experience a loving atitude which closes the gap between himself and the world without leading him away from the newly discovered objects. This whole pattern remains as the child grows and learns from his parents and family more and about persons and things and is encouraged to perceive connections between them and extend the elements of his home relations to these new objects.

Basic to this "extending" function is an atmosphere of harmony among the members of the family, especially the parents. Common agreement on values and special functions conditions a child's attitude toward persons and things long before he can reason about them.

The *orienting* task consists in helping the child to place a properly human imprint on the initially unconscious, non-rational roots he has developed. He is guided so that he *understands* the meaning of personal relationships—how he is to live with his parents, his brothers and sisters; how he is to contribute to a life in a community; how he is to use and live in the home; which are the things he is especially to value. Parents prepare the way for the child's understanding of the world in which he lives—its requirements of order and discipline—and the choices it will demand. In other words, parents orient the child's activities, helping him to bring the growing rational powers of knowledge and love to bear upon their non-rational forms.

Intellectual awakening is encouraged by profiting from such devices as "why" questions, small discussions on the basis of daily incidents. Excessive television viewing and comic-magazine reading are avoided, and more is asked from the child's creative abilities in art, games, etc. Reflection is linked to decisions and actions. Parents begin by exemplifying energy in the decisions they take before the child; a wavering parental attitude is often introjected in an individual, causing later weakness in his ability to decide. Parents are conscious of the need for having children establish inner controls of behavior. In virtue of a loving relationship the mother makes the child understand that there are things he may *want* and that it is perfectly understandable that he may want them, but that he may not have them because of their effects. Much repetition may be required, but she perseveres kindly, until the child introjects the feeling of a loving mother who does not want him to play, let us say, with breakable glasses. Later he will be led to understand why. The habit once established provides an inner control and contributes to the kind of liberty that will be encouraged as his rational powers develop—liberty in its "prolonging" meaning. In this case, his freedom prolongs a decision previously adopted: that not everything one wants may be had, even though the "wanting" is still felt and cannot be rejected.

The experience of customs and manners within the family helps the child to overcome selfish forms of attachment. For example, the boy, observing that Father thanks Mother for every service, learns the meaning of respect and consideration for others. Mother and Father both give the example of generous interest in each other's activities and those of the children.

The love and harmony between parents makes it possible for them to make demands upon the children without producing an atmosphere of authoritarianism. The children know that there is an order in the house which is treasured because it makes the people living there happy. They know that if they break it their parents have the right to ask for reparation. Experiences of right order belong to the essence of education and must be considered as such.

Education of the personality requires the child to absorb both unconsciously and consciously a sense of personal worth. This may be increased, for example, by the cultivation of a proper acceptance of sex and the sex role. Oraison says it is important that no spiritual or ritualistic fear should attend the discovery of sex difference, which takes place around the third or fourth year of life of the child.[6] It is also necessary that the discovery be accepted without any feeling of inferiority or superiority. Boys and girls each have their proper roles and responsibilities and should receive praise or correction in accordance with this fact. Co-operation between boys and girls should also be practiced in the home environment, a co-

[6] Oraison, *op. cit.,* p. 91.

operation which will be characteristic of successful social relations in their later life.

This is the family. Within it we find the individual living—
when conditions are as described—in the threefold context of
relationships to persons, to ideas and values, and to the home
itself. These relationships advance dynamically from the stage
of strong instinctive emotional attachments to bonds which
elevate the non-rational forms of love into a love enlightened
by the intellect and in living interaction with freedom. Within
the family, the child is initiated in his education for freedom
and develops his first personal desire for truth and goodness.
And this education will lead him gradually to the independence
in thought and action which he needs in order to cope, without the danger of absorption, with the drastically changing
modern world.

Unfortunately this kind of family is far from being a universal reality. Hence the need not only for an institution to
complete the family's work but, in view of the many cases in
which the family's work has been wholly inadequate, an institution which offers a substitute.

The School. As an educational institution the school is
ordinarily set up with a view to carrying further the educational work begun in the family. However, given the problems
of the modern family, we may also see the school as a potential
agency in providing needed substitutes for deficient family
education. Personal relationships issue from connections between teacher and students and between the students themselves. Ties with nature as a whole are furthered through the
school curriculum and activities, while the school's physical
structure and its peculiar atmosphere add the feeling of
"home." Finally, the school's values—what is called "its philosophy" plus the world of ideas embodied in the curriculum—

extend the individual's ideological ties. On the other hand, the school, in its mode of teaching, can place emphasis upon the integration of human powers and provide opportunities for children to develop their ability to reflect, to love, and to act freely.

Let us examine, first of all, what the school does for human rootedness (keeping in mind that it never supplants the work of the family). The main personal relationship is, of course, that between teacher and students. Circumstances make this relationship differ, depending on the amount of time the teacher spends with a class and his personal influence. Given the conditions of society in our day, it is wise to encourage the presence of a teacher who is able to come closer to a class (for example, the home-room teacher). Such teachers need to be selected with much care, with regard to their character traits, the mastery of their subject, and their effectiveness in teaching. Personal relationships in school depend to a large degree on the sense that a child has not only of the kindness and love of his teacher, but also of his knowledge, of the interest he awakens in teaching. Only then does he feel there is someone really "great" before him.

A teacher placed in a position of influence needs first of all to establish his authority. This is especially important at the grade-school level. Children easily sense weak points in a teacher and often try him out in the first classes. Once he has gained their respect by a gentle but firm exercise of authority, educational efforts in a free and spontaneous atmosphere can develop.

The teacher strives to know his class. He is aware that he is bound to encounter the negative traits of contemporary society in one form or another among his pupils. And so he uses all available means for gaining insight into the structure of the class: observation, conversation, the many available guidance techniques and services.

The teacher, like any good educator, profits from the educational value of love; through love he awakens the creative energies of the student, his interest, enthusiasm, and desire for knowledge. He is also careful to make his demands conform to the potentialities of the students, not to fall below them or reach too far above them. Finally, knowing the connection between love and liberty, he is careful to utilize his relation with the class to provide opportunities for initiative, free decision, and action.

The school is a *community that educates* more than a place where instruction is given. In this sense it embodies as a whole the teacher-student relationship described. It re-enacts the relations in the family structure where each person in his proper function educates through personal contacts. Like the family the school possesses a set of commitments, values, and beliefs. These form the bases on which the students may satisfy their need for ideological roots. It was Dewey's insight into this human need that made him, in spite of his relativism, place such emphasis upon the democratic faith as the ideological setting of his school. And in this stress upon some ideological commitment in the school we may well learn from him.

Students find their ideological roots through the experiential contact with the school atmosphere as they do in the family; they also find them in their contact with the ideological treasury of humanity given in the curriculum. Their own activities—reflection, discussion, study—are means given to analyze them objectively and personally incorporate their values.

The school as a community which provides not only for student-teacher interaction and for ideological roots, but also

for effective student-student relations is all the more a family
—that is, a center of roots—if it is a home for the individual.
And we see home in the meaning we gave it earlier, as a
personalized contact with the world of nature. The school as
a home brings the individual to a personal love of his country
and widens his horizon to feelings of contact with the whole
cosmos. And this can be reached through accurate and scientific knowledge, vividly presented.

In view of what we have seen as the responsibility of the
present-day educator, the family structure of the school should
be stressed above organization, buildings, and techniques,
which, though necessary, are subordinate to the greater goal
of the school: the imparting of knowledge and the aid given
to the development of personality. To an alarming extent,
many of today's students will have had no previous experience
of education in a family setting, and to implement it we need
to use all our resources, creativity and ingenuity.

In the atmosphere above described, attention is paid to the
pressing need of the times: education of stable, balanced per-
sonalities. The attainment of such qualities is not something
that can be taught; but it can be furthered by the mode of
teaching. Here are some suggestions.

First of all, be clear about the goals of this education. In
sum they are: to utilize the dynamism of group action so that
the student may progressively integrate and harmonize his
powers in terms of ideals and commitments; to help him reach
the ability to think and to act not by intellectual pressure or
other compulsion, and much less out of conformity, but in
freedom and love. Finally, to help him see his life and activity
in terms of a task, a goal with immediate and future consequences.

Secondly, have a clearly conceived idea of the means for

achieving these goals. The individual's ability to think is grounded in knowledge; not so much knowledge of isolated facts as an intellectual synthesis which is the personal possession of each student and in relation to which he is integrated. Hence, lay stress on this personal grasp. Understanding is often secured through illustrations, through bringing all the senses to bear upon the material to be assimilated. Visual and auditory aids have thus an important place, but not to the extent that intellectual functions are impaired.

Evaluations of the student's proficiency should be made not according to "text-book repetition ability" but in terms of his ability to integrate the material presented to him and perhaps to elaborate new thoughts from what he has studied and read. (This technique is not to be limited to college activities; even grade schools can profit from the approach in a way adapted to the age of the students.) Motivation, appeal to interests, to affective powers in students is important. It is also important to know how to communicate enthusiasm; a good means is to re-enact the process by which the teacher himself came to grasp the matter to be learned. The relation of personal anecdotes when teaching history, literature and abstract materials such as philosophy, and even mathematics, can be helpful. Most important is to rely less and less on static course outlines, on memorization. All these things have been suggested by educators many times, but it is essential to know their importance not only for the mere purpose of order and interest, but as implementing the knowledge that widens the scope for reflection.

Decision-making ability is helped, as we have often said, by the opportunities provided for initiative and creativity. Extra-curricular activities often offer such opportunities: discussion groups, school government, etc. Within the class community there should also be areas for initiative and decisions (we shall later offer a concrete example when we speak of education through ideals). Even when one is teaching composition one can see to it that students *choose,* and do not simply accept, the phrases that will best express their meaning. Class discussions, encouraging sensible questions and objections, provide means for educating the individual in his ability to reflect and take intellectual positions.

There is another element related to this education for decision-making ability and responsible action: preparing the individual to endure loneliness. By "loneliness" is meant the isolation that a person experiences when "swimming against the current." Students should know that they are apt to meet this in an atmosphere of conformity or one in which the majority differs from them in matters of belief. Nevertheless they are prepared for it by experiencing the importance of having objective opinions and of adhering firmly to, and even struggling for, one's views if one has real reasons to believe these views are sound. Thus healthy tensions in the classroom are encouraged. But simultaneously, respect for the opinions of others, objectivity in judgment, ability to recognize personal errors and to praise others for their qualities is also encouraged. All these factors contribute to leading the individual to participate rightly in community life and at the same time to build a valuable community.

These thoughts must bring to an end our treatment of the task of education in aiding man at the natural level to develop himself as an integrated being and a self-sufficient personality. We have seen that this is possible to a large extent in the family and school as educational communities. This education has two phases, one resting on the other. The first is to provide the means for satisfying an individual's need for roots as given in persons, ideas, and "home." The importance of the family as the center of all primary human roots makes it a task of the times for education as a whole, and particularly education in schools, to adopt the structure of the family. Against this background, the second task of education is to develop in the student the ability to integrate all his non-rational and rational activities and especially to become able to love, to reflect and to act freely. This second aim is to prepare the individual to cope with a "mass society" and to create a true community informed by a living, personal, and unselfish love.

In connection with all we have said regarding natural integration it is interesting to note what a psychoanalyst has to say about education after studying clinically the problems posed by brainwashing techniques in totalitarian settings and in the environment of contemporary mass civilization. Here are some of his reflections:

We have to inform the authorities of the existing unobtrusive pressure currents in our actual world, for they are not limited to totalitarian countries alone and they may have a weakening effect on the personality. These new universal circumstances make the human personality more sensitive and vulnerable toward mental contagion from without. Education to conformity does not strengthen individual morale either. . . . When the emphasis is on facts and more facts without the ethos and moral commitment behind them, the school as a fact-factory unobtrusively prints its conformity on the student. Mere knowledge of facts does not strengthen the soul.

The question of individual morale and mental backbone is a problem of education both in the family and in the schools. Modern psychology and especially psychoanalysis believe in the deeply rooted *vertical* education, starting in the nursery and continuing into personal relations and identifications with educators and leaders. Our technical age of *horizontalism* makes people feel lost, without relations.

.   .   .   .

One can be sure that in a free, democratic form of government a system of different rules and controls has to develop to check the imprisoned thinking and narrowed psychic development provoked by unilateral political infection and mental contagion. Freedom to think for oneself has to be more highly stimulated than ever. Schools have to promote the student's personal initiative to develop new thoughts. It is not only a question of ego strength but also one of how to protect the principle of freedom and independence in a developing personality. . . .

.   .   .   .

Man has to battle inwardly for every new insight. . . . His inner strength and mental backbone depend on a free, unlimited knowledge of himself and on man's simple self-confidence that he or his heirs eventually will reach that goal. It depends on his unfrustrated belief in human values and on his awareness of belonging to a group of other people, who like him and have esteem for him. It depends, too, on his education in both freedom and self-discipline.[7]

In spite of the importance of the above, every effort at the natural level and with natural purposes only, essential though such efforts are, is necessarily partial and incomplete (as evident through our study of naturalism). Therefore, everything that has been said in this regard must be related to what will follow.

EDUCATION AND NATURAL-SUPERNATURAL INTEGRATION

The complete goal of Christian education in our times is to form a man who in terms of the integrity of his being is

[7] Joost A. M. Mérloo, "Brainwashing and Menticide," *Identity and Anxiety: Survival of the Person in Mass Society,* ed. Maurice Stein et al. (Glencoe, Illinois: The Free Press, 1960), pp. 518–520.

thoroughly committed in a living faith to God; and who in virtue of this commitment is conscious of his instrumentality and the task he is to perform as a member of the Christian community, of the Mystical Body of Christ. Hence we see the task of completing the formation of man in the supernatural dimension of his existence under two aspects: the ways by which we can assist the individual in becoming receptive to grace and an increase in a living faith in, and relationship to, the person of God; and the ways by which we can help him become aware of his personal and time-conditioned task.

The Conditions for a Living Faith

A life of faith means the elevation of an individual's entire being and all his activities to a higher order in which he finds a new type of rootedness. The clue as to how we may help him achieve this—or rather, prepare him for a fruitful increase of grace—lies in the recognition of the analogical relation and the real psychological affinity or deep unity between roots in the natural order and roots in the supernatural world. And this analogical relation, coupled with the philosophic and theological concept of secondary causality and the mediating character of creatures, suggests an educational method worth exploring.

Every one of the basic human contacts has the power of providing experiences which condition the understanding of supernatural realities and really lead to the supernatural world, or union with God. In other words, the experience of roots or felt connections at the natural level helps man find his place in the supernatural order; and moreover, these connections, when they issue from the kind of human activities and attitudes which serve to unite the soul with God, really in themselves accomplish this end.

Let us begin by examining the analogical connection between natural and supernatural experiences. We have said that it is essential for the natural integrity of man's being that he bring all his activities (rational and non-rational) to bear upon the objects to which he is naturally related, and that this is made possible through interiorized bonds to persons, ideas, and home (as a symbolic expression of the connections between man and nature as a whole). We have seen that this is most adequately fulfilled in the family, and it is also in the family that we find the best natural analogy of our roots in supernatural realities.

In the family the main relationship is of a social nature: the relationship between the child and his parents and brothers and sisters as a group relationship, and the relationship between the child and each one of the persons in the family as a person-to-person relationship. If we remember what was said in our preceding chapter with regard to the meaning of faith as the contact of a person with a Person, we shall understand why all psychologists are bringing out evidence that disturbances in the religious life of individuals, distortions in their beliefs about and experiences of God, are very often due to the lack of genuine and rightly ordered personal contacts in the family. We shall also understand why Mouroux, when dealing with faith, refers us to St. Augustine's study of the structure of belief, which was based on the primitive and irreplaceable experience of persons in the family, in friendship and in the state (*De fide rerum quae non videntur*, P.L., XL, 171-174).[8]

Most important is the father-experience, since it is the chief

[8] Mouroux, *I Believe*, p. 58.

conditioning factor of our image of God and of our relationship to Him. When we try to explain the main attribute of God—that He is a Father moved essentially by love, who has greater care for us than for the lilies of the fields or the birds of the air—to a person whose only experience is of a neglectful father or an extremely authoritarian one, we find ourselves confronted with an almost insurmountable barrier. One often hears something like this comment of a well-educated man to a priest-psychologist: "How can I say the *Our Father* when I had a father like mine?" Hence the child stands in need of father-experiences which resemble, even if imperfectly, those he develops with God. He must feel that the authority and love of his father are a powerful source of security; he must learn about the omnipresence and personal care of God through awareness, especially in his early life, of the presence of his father and of his father's real interest in his activities.

The mother-experience offers, on the other hand, a different facet of the divine image: the kindness and tenderness, the absolute generosity of the God who says: "Can a woman forget her infant, so as not to have pity on the son of her womb? And if she should forget, yet will not I forget thee. Behold I have graven thee in my hands" (Isaias 49:15-16).

Experiences in the family such as we described when referring to natural integration are predisposing experiences for an understanding of the personal roots in God that everyone must attain and for the mode of our relationship to God. An outstanding example of this is found in the life of St. Thérèse of Lisieux and the peculiar quality of her way to sainthood. As Hans Urs von Balthasar explains:

Everything that Thérèse achieves at the supernatural level is rooted in something she has experienced at the natural level.

Nothing moved her more, perhaps, than the experience of being loved by her father and mother; consequently her picture of God is colored by a child's love. And it is to Louis and Zélie Martin that we owe the doctrine of the "little way" and of "spiritual childhood," for they allowed the God who is more than father and mother to find a dwelling in the heart of Thérèse.[9]

There is also an analogical relationship between the children's relations among themselves in the family and with their parents, and the experience of the communion of all the faithful in Christ and the universal fatherhood of God. The family atmosphere provides the experiential context for the quality of our beliefs; the idea we have of divine authority, love, justice, mercy and truth, and our concept of what our obedience, respect, and love should be depend on the way we have personally lived out these ideas in the intimacy of our family. The attitudes of the family (and, to a great extent, of the school) toward every created object—above all, the way in which they present nature in its wonders, the achievements of men throughout history in the fields of the arts, science, and technology—prove to be a powerful aid to the individual's discovery of God in these things. Teilhard de Chardin once said that he owed much to his mother for his overwhelming desire to find Christ hidden in the mysterious forces of the earth.

Family life is always centered and situated somewhere, in a place and a home. Here we find synthesized the whole of the family relationships, its customs and its beliefs, and this whole analogically represents the entire world of Christian belief as it is centered in God and visibly embodied in the Church, its tradition, its structure, and its customs. It is in the home, the roots in a place which man needs, that he is able to experience very early the immense treasures of life within the Church, his supernatural home: his close familial bonds with God the

[9] Hans Urs von Balthasar, Thérèse of Lisieux, p. 76.

Father, with Christ, the Blessed Virgin and the saints; the life
of grace communicated by the sacraments and all the signs
and sacramentals by which Christian beliefs are nurtured.
Recalling his early home experiences, Jean Guitton conveys
to us not only the analogical relation between these and his
experiences of the supernatural order but also the actual deep
unity between them at this period of life:

Religion is mixed up with the essential feelings which will form
the personality. It is because they know and feel these bonds that
mothers make their children take part in the actions of faith at
the same time as they learn life's first lessons, so that faith and
life shall spring from the same source. The sensation of being, of
being loved and of believing thus become one and the same.

. . . .

The Catholic child escapes an imprisoned mentality. Father Christmas lives on, but as the symbol of a lasting truth, the truth of a
bountiful God, friend of simple folk, and more than ever on these
cold dark days. It is the same with family rites. Father, mother,
little brother, the table, bread, bed, the front door, the visitor to
the house, the spelling-book—the sign of the cross, hands joined,
gaze heavenwards—hymns, priest, mass, host on the tongue: these
are all one world, not two distinct ones. The distinction between
heaven and earth does not exist, still less that between immanence
and transcendence.[10]

The above quotation brings us to the second aspect we have
distinguished in our treatment of the ways to a living faith: the
relationship between the two orders is not merely analogical,
but one order *really* leads to the other, and both are conceived
as united in one experience. To achieve or help achieve this
real connection it is well to consider a sort of double law which
governs the relation between the natural and supernatural
orders when they are referred to man as a situated being. This

10 Jean Guitton, "The Catholic Home, Source of Life and Faith,"
Lumen Vitae, VII (April–June, 1952), 215–216.

double law has its metaphysical root in the power of secondary causality possessed by all creatures, and its psychological root in the tendency in man to experience union with the invisible through the visible (*"Per amorem visibilium ad amorem invisibilium rapiamur"*). Its double directionality points to what we may call a law of donation, or conveyance, and a law of transmission. In the first case, we say that God *gives* or conveys something of His attributes, of His power, His goodness, and His wisdom, to creatures, while on the other hand, man is able to give to creatures the whole of the love, respect, and obedience he owes to God. In virtue of the mediating character of creatures, what God has given to them is transmitted to man; and on the other hand, what man has given to them is transmitted to God.[11] It is evident, of course, that all natural mediators are participating in the mediating role of Christ. We can represent the process graphically as follows:

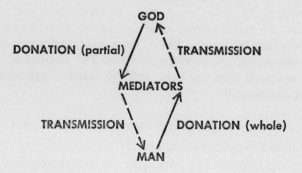

[11] Father Joseph Kentenich, founder of the Schoenstatt Movement, used two German expressions for these laws: *Uebertragung* ("donation") and *Weiterleitung* ("transmission"). The literal translation of *Uebertragung* is "transference," but we render it "donation" here because of the quite different meaning which "transference" has in psychoanalysis. Donation on God's part is partial; for man it can be whole.

What this means in practice is that if we foster right relationships in the natural order and help those whom we educate to see God through the objects of these relationships, they will really lead to God, and we shall have a natural-supernatural relationship or organism of bonds. Thus, once again, not only is there an analogy between the love that a child has for his father and his love of God, there is also a genuine means of finding God *in* the natural forms of filial love. The task of education is, then, to assist the individual's progress from a non-rational experience of the unity between natural and supernatural things to a conscious recognition that all natural things, inasmuch as they participate in some of the attributes of God, have a mediating value. And here one distinguishes a hierarchy of mediators as well as a connection between these mediators. Persons are mediators *par excellence* because they can become conscious of their function—all other things are in a sense subordinated to them. They can see to it that the individual is really led through their natural relationships to God. And the closer the person is to God, the better will he perform the operation. This brings us to the *educator*.

The realization that all created things participate in the perfections and attributes of God and that we are therefore able to bring them all that we owe to God (donation), coupled with the realization that these things are at the same time so many steppingstones leading us to God and leading God to us (transmission) is the crux of life in the world as a mature Christian. There are two main ways by which the educator can bring us to this realization: by his being and by his activities.

First of all, the educator fulfills this aim by *his person* and the atmosphere he creates with it. He has experienced at some time of his life genuine natural rootedness, and through this experience he has been able to find his roots in God. There is, for instance, little fruit to be expected from a teacher dominated by a view of God exclusively as Judge, for he will probably mediate it in terms of an authoritarian attitude.

The educator is himself aware of the mediating role of things; he realizes that a minimum of natural roots and bonds are prerequisites for experiences of God, and that they really lead to God. His attitude is best expressed by the word *priesthood* as qualified by the traits of "fatherhood" and "motherhood." Every one of the faithful in the Church is called to share in a "spiritual-real priesthood," and hence in the mediating role of the priesthood of Jesus Christ.[12] Such priesthood belongs in a privileged way to the educator. However, it belongs more specifically (because of the sacramental bond) to parents than to teachers. Thus it is evident that any educator who is called to complete or substitute for the work of parents must, if he is to be adequate to his task, embody a spiritual fatherhood and motherhood as intrinsically united to his priestly character.

In virtue of the above, everything that was said regarding the analogy between the earthly fatherhood and motherhood and the divine applies here. The educator strives to be consistent and firm in his decisions and to provide security and peace, as a mediator of divine immutability; he tries to show solicitude as mediator of divine providence; he is both loving and just, but just because he loves, and he strives for holiness in virtue of the holiness of God. He is selfless, kind, and loyal as a mother, communicating to the educand divine love, goodness, and fidelity.

[12] Cf. Yves M. J. Congar, O.P., *Lay People in the Church*, trans. Donald Attwater (Westminster, Maryland: Newman Press, 1957), p. 180.

The educator not only strives to lead the individual through natural bonds to God through his being; he does so also through his *activities*. In the first place we may consider the active encounter between the educator and educand. Everything that was said about it at the natural level is valid here, and there is in addition the supernatural orientation to be considered. The educator's function is to prepare the individual to feel free, on the strength of a personal orientation to and confrontation with God, to engage himself totally in the activities of the world to which he may be called; concretely, this means freedom to expend one's energies, all the powers of one's being, in the pursuit of one's tasks—whether manual or intellectual, scientific or metaphysical—and in the private activities dealing with persons. The educator's respect and confidence ultimately hinge on the fact that the child is an image of God. He tries to awaken trust and love in the child in order to begin the direct task of transmitting the hidden significance of things. It is easier to bring little children to see God in things, for they are more receptive to religious values than are their elders. Many means are available for working in the first grades in this task. For example, a teacher reported having had the class center all its work for decorating the classroom upon these general ideas: "All the Works of the Lord Bless the Lord" and "A List of Lovely Things." For the first idea, the children searched all over for old leaves and pebbles and shells; some brought insect collections, nuts, and seeds. All the while, the class was talking about using their eyes, looking around for the things God has made and being attentive to what He wants to say through them. With regard to the second idea, the children searched for things which, though common, revealed some unusual and perhaps ordinarily unnoticed beauty. The children wrote about them and painted them and pondered what message they might bring from God.

Working with adolescents, the educator keeps in mind that their greater receptivity is to ethical rather than to religious values and that their rational capacities are growing. A teacher can for this reason bring them to connect certain ethical ideals with divine perfections. In initiating the study of sociology, for example, a teacher may profit from his perception of the student's concern about the social and economic repercussions of some recent political event. He refers this concern to such economic factors as natural resources and social activity. From here he moves on to the elements of a just order. He traces the idea of justice back to God and explains how God has brought it into society—how temporal things are provided with one or another of the divine attributes; how these things are structured in an order which allows each one to enjoy this order according to his needs; and how this just distribution of temporal things, because it is a representation of God's Justice, leads to God. This approach may help the pupil to see a connection between our concern for temporal affairs and God, and between our ties with society, nature, and ideas as expressed in the notion of "justice" and God. This attitude can be reinforced through discussions or questions; the whole approach, however, should never suggest any compromise between the religious and the temporal which diminishes the authenticity of the temporal: we should avoid taking pragmatically a "Catholic approach" in our teaching. What we have to do is develop the belief that we *can* lend ourselves wholly to the pursuit of truth in any field with its proper means and methods, confident that the God who is truth will be discovered through our work and that we will thus be led to Him.

But the educator not only shows his students the image of

God in things, or helps them to find Him, he also speaks directly about Him, and about the Blessed Virgin, the saints and all other supernatural realities. The small child learns that to reach heaven is something like coming home; he learns that as he loves his father and mother he must also love God and Our Lady. He sees himself as growing along with the Child Jesus. There is a nice set of pictures of the Child Jesus' "growing-up" life which can be found in the children's room of some Catholic families. Something like this is an aid to the understanding we must all reach that we are born in Christ and Christ lives in us.

In all of these activities, however, the educator realizes his limitations. He knows that the connection between natural and supernatural experiences is only analogical, and that if he does not acknowledge, for example, his limitations as a father, the child, discovering them later on, will project this image of an imperfect father upon God; and this either because he has been taught to see God in his father or has unconsciously developed the connection. The task that the educator has is that of striving for personal holiness and trying to exemplify the traits of God for his educand, but he must also realize that he is human, and his errors and limitations must be courageously acknowledged before his educand. This attitude balances the one which lays stress on the mediating nature of educational influences. Oraison asserts that if children perceive, for example, that their parents are reasonable people who are *trying* to be just, and therefore recognize their mistakes, they will develop deep confidence in them; for the parents' admission that they fall short of absolute justice confirms for the children the existence of the absolute standard of justice of a truly transcendental order. Through the father who acknowledges his mistakes the way is thus open for that Father who does not make mistakes and who so loves us as to give His Son to save the world.[13]

These last observations bring home to us the truth that not only do we need those natural experiences which are related by analogy to our relations with God and thus condition our roots in supernatural reality but we need also those *contrast* experiences which prove to us the insufficiency of natural means and show the transcendence of God. The way by contrast complements the way by roots, and we as educators can further it by pointing precisely to the limitations of natural roots.

A final point regarding the activities by which the educator can lead to God: he must make clear that, above all, personal bonds demand sacrifice, that little mortifications born out of love increase love, and that these are God's especially favored means of drawing us to Him. Thus, in all natural attachments there is an element of sacrifice, of renunciation, that also, and very properly, leads to God.

Education of the Christian Person in His Time-Conditioned Mission

While we are trying to re-establish the natural and supernatural roots of human existence in Catholic education it is important to lay stress on the values of Christian responsibility and engagement, to teach the individual to recognize the nature of his Christian vocation. The first element mentioned—stress on Christian responsibility and engagement—presupposes an education for *Christian freedom*.

The education for Christian freedom involves everything that we have noted with regard to freedom as an instrument

[13] Oraison, *op. cit.,* p. 135.

for natural integration. Beyond this, however, it calls for us to see the full meaning of freedom as the most precious condition for accepting and living in faith, and as a gift of God which He infinitely values.

With the foregoing in mind, let us reflect on some aspects of this education for freedom. We can begin by noting the role which God intends freedom to play in His plan of salvation. The commandments state the minimum which is required from us. He gives us also a number of controls to help us reach perfection: His desires expressed in the evangelical counsels, His interior communications through the Holy Spirit and the outward manifestation of His will in temporal events. The Church herself exemplifies this method, for she has traditionally allowed room in the context of her organization and authority for the individual—the private sphere. She leaves to the individual not only the right but the duty to make decisions regarding things which are not immediately controlled by her authority. She recognizes in everyone a charisma, a special vocation which must be accomplished, and she allows scope for freedom in its realization. That she lets the initiative for the development and deepening of the Christian life come from below—that is, from the ordinary sphere of Christian life—is shown by the variety of the movements and kinds of spirituality which flourish in her midst.

This method of God and of His Church is all the more necessary in times when the individual must face situations for which he is not prepared, for which he has "not been told what to do." It is reflected in a principle expressed and applied in the Schoenstatt Movement, whose educational orientation we have been drawing upon: freedom stressed as much as possible, external controls as few as possible; but an education *for* freedom and decision in an atmosphere of a generous love for

God as strong as possible.[14] There is nothing essentially new about this principle except the realization that the specific individuality of a mature individual, and hence of a mature Christian, is proportionate to the number of internal controls he has. The maturity entails a greater number of actions done not under external pressure, but either because of a dominant habit (in the sense of decisions made to prolong this habit), or as the result of decisions, taken after careful reflection, which represent a break with the past. And because of the intimate connection between freedom and love, it also means that the individual, as a supernaturalized being, will produce actions informed by charity—the love of God in Himself and the love of God in all things.

The educator will be aware of course, in practicing this principle, that smaller children need a greater number of external controls; but he tries to see that these become internalized, and accomplishes this by his loving attitude and by bringing the child into relation with the Person of God. He understands freedom to be precisely the ability to develop controls by which our impulses may be governed (not suppressed) in view of a Person who loves us. The educator realizes that, in general, his tutelage will eventually become superfluous, but he hopes to leave in the unconscious and the conscious mind of his educand, along with the security afforded by his love, the knowledge of ultimate truths, the general principles and values of life, and, above all, the example of a life oriented by faith in and love of God. These are the inner controls for the Christian life, and they make freedom meaningful.

[14] Alex Menningen, "Gruendzuege einer pastoralen Paedagogik," *Neue Schoepfung,* ed. Heinrich Maria Koester (Limburg: Lahn-Verlag, 1948), p. 571.

In educating adolescents for Christian freedom, especially with regard to their spiritual lives, the educator avoids stressing too much what are considered the minimum requirements and accentuates the higher possibilities which may be realized; he profits in this respect from what is magnanimous, generous and idealistic in youth.

The educator embodies also in his education for freedom the almost unlimited confidence that God has in us. Thus, in encouraging decision and initiative, he even risks faulty or wrong choices on the part of the student, trusting that if he provides the proper environment these will eventually be recognized as erroneous by the subject. The following example illustrates what is meant:

In a particular family of very strong practicing Christians and of a high level of culture and education the eldest of the five children, a youth of between seventeen and eighteen years of age, announced one day that he had lost the Faith, that he would never again set foot inside a church nor take part in any religious services or practices, for to him, henceforth they would mean nothing more than hypocritical shams. In the face of an obviously calm and clear set of mind, his parents by mutual consent decided that it would be a better thing to say nothing and to respect this crisis. Never once on a Sunday, despite the strongest desire to do so, did his mother venture to say: "Will you come to Mass with us?" Throughout the course of many years, while continuing to live their own daily Christian life as sincerely as possible, the parents had the united and very uncommon courage never to bear down in any way on the conscience of the young man. Outwardly nothing was happening: then, when he was about twenty-six years of age and had just completed a brilliant course of university study, he announced that after mature reflection he had made up his mind to enter a Benedictine monastery. To his astonished parents he added the comment: "I can tell you now that if you had not shown the respect for my liberty of judgment that you did I don't know if I should have ever found the Faith again."[15]

What is most important when laying such stress on freedom is to foster an atmosphere in which the individual can develop a certain delicacy of perception which will enable him to sense in the moment what is right and pleasing to God, or to recognize faults or mistakes later on. It is an atmosphere of love and union with God which purifies the unconscious more than restrictions, however necessary these may be, and forms the moral and religious conscience of the mature Christian.

When one speaks of education for freedom, the problem of the rightful place of authority always emerges. To reach an intelligent recognition of the authority of the Church, to be able to accept authorities at other levels of life, it is important that the individual should perceive experientially the connection between freedom and authority through the mediation of love. The virtue involved here is obedience; and it is well to see charity as the form and soul of obedience. With this connection clear, the educator bound in charity to his educand has the right to demand obedience. Such demands are necessary as experiential conditions for attitudes which will be called for throughout life but which are especially important before God. A challenge to obedience which rests on charity entails some of the confidence God has in man; it means that I call for your obedience "because I know you *can* do it, and I *trust* you will do it."

A child who experiences obedience associated with his love for a person and this person's love for him will not have much difficulty in understanding and fulfilling the essence of the Christian life: the loving and free submission of the will to

[15] Oraison, *op. cit.*, pp. 77–78.

God and to those here on earth who represent Him. Urs von Balthasar again sees this truth exemplified in the life of St. Thérèse. He points out that her relationship to God and her unconditional surrender to His will was always grounded on her personal love for Him (the way of spiritual childhood). And he adds that this attitude found its first support in the contact with her parents. For Thérèse to be good means only to do the will of her father and give joy to her mother, and Urs von Balthasar wonders whether Thérèse was an exception or "whether similar effects would not be produced in most children (who would love God in a personal way and without fear) if only parents showed children deeper Christian love and humility."[16]

To understand obedience in its connection with charity and charity as connected with freedom is to see no inherent opposition between freedom and obedience. It is important to see obedience not as passive submission but as active and free love, leaving room for initiative and personal decisions. To educate for this type of obedience is of great moment, since the mass trends of society in their bearing on the Christian life contain the danger of producing a passive Christian, a "Church collectivist" which Rahner likens to the herd-men in Dostoievsky's Legend of the Great Inquisitor.[17] We do not want a Christianity of "yes-men," but one which in its obedience to authority is moved on the natural level by reflection and voluntary decision and supernaturally by charity.

The main task of an education for Christian freedom can thus be summarized as follows: the help given to the individual in

[16] Urs von Balthasar, *op. cit.*, p. 77.
[17] Karl Rahner, S.J., "Der Einzelne in der Kirche," *Stimmen der Zeit*, CXXXIX (1946–1947), 271. See also: Frederich Heer, "The Rebirth of Catholic Obedience," *Cross Currents*, VI (Spring, 1956), 119–130.

developing a dominant attitude which integrates all his past decisions as they have resulted through natural contacts and as they are informed by his own supernatural orientation. It aims at a dominant attitude which is essentially religious insofar as religion is the living bond between man and all his human activities and God. Future decisions will either strengthen or weaken this attitude. But the goal of this education is also to help the individual become aware of the creative element in freedom, of the possibility of an action which will totally, or at least to a great extent, change the course of his life. Both these tasks are accomplished in the family and the school by a favorable environment, by the stimulation given to the establishment of inner controls and supernaturally oriented habits and, above all, by the opportunities provided for initiative and decisions.

Education for Christian freedom is the conditioning factor in the preparation we give the individual for his Christian mission. And this preparation consists in making our students aware of their membership and of their special task within the Christian community. In this respect Congar asserts that the task of the educator or priest is to give the individuals whom they educate "an over-all view of God's design for the world, to help them to find their place in that design and to learn what is the Christian's service and responsibility in the world."[18] Such a task can best be performed through the dynamic interchange of group action. We shall return to this later when we refer to a practical means by which we may further the entire education of the Christian personality. For the moment, we shall limit ourselves to a few general considerations.

Preparation for the Christian mission as a whole begins, as

[18] Congar, *op. cit.*, p. 411.

does every other phase of education, with the family. The family lets the child experience the meaning of working for the community by giving him some special task, pointing out that doing this task means making a little contribution to the "big treasury" in the Church community from which anyone in need may draw. Family worship helps the child to grasp the meaning of the offering of Christ's sacrifice *with the whole* family, and hence the whole Mystical Body.

In school a later rational understanding of the tasks to be performed in time is prepared, for instance, by the work of the class in expectation of some liturgical feast, in contributions to mission work, or in the many varied tasks performed in common by the class or the school as a whole. Generally speaking, every course with its special subject matter offers an incentive to awakening responsibility for the task to which an individual may later be called in his profession or special field of interests. Curriculum subjects also offer material for discussions concerning the needs and situations of society and of the Church. However, in a normal teaching situation it is often not possible to provide more than a general orientation regarding the Christian mission, and very little can be said about every individual's personal task. Hence the wisdom, especially in high school, of having some time especially allotted to discussions of this type. It is important, of course, that such discussions be carried out in a spirit of seriousness and guided by the teacher who is nearer to the class and who knows it better.

How can such discussions be approached? Congar points out that it is well to start with an over-all view of God's design for the world (something which should already be covered by the class in religion). It is important that every individual reach an understanding of the meaning of instrumentality. On this basis a description of the situation of the times and of the role of the Church with regard to it can be given in terms of mutual interchange between teacher and students. These discussions should be brought down, as far as possible, to the concrete sphere of life and action of the students.

In respect to our times it is wise to see to it that the problems which we have discussed in the first chapters of this book be considered in one way or another by students in high school and college. At the college level there should be, especially for those who will enter the teaching profession, an opportunity to view these problems in relation to educational activities. Discussions of this sort, we believe, should have a part in one or another of the required courses (preferably philosophy of education). If we are to contribute a remedy to the contemporary situation, teacher training should include a presentation of the problems posed by conformity and mass trends in Western civilization (discussions and reading are fruitful aids).

Over and above what has been said, there is one further attitude which it is important to foster in Catholic education if awareness of our problems and of the task which devolves on the Christian is to be translated into action and the impetus given for courageous struggle against difficulties. This is what we call "practical faith in divine providence." Faith in divine providence rests on the perception of the divine presence and divine activity in the order of the universe, in the structure of things, in the commandments, and, concretely, in current temporal events. It includes, in this last meaning, the ability to decipher the design of God in things and to believe practically that God will guide us in whatever we do to further this plan. To implement this attitude is to exhort and encourage our students by word and example to acquire a fine perception of the presence of God in daily happenings, to reflect on the actions we feel these happenings call for and to make decisions in their regard.

Faith in divine providence requires us to be convinced of its time-conditioned meaning as an aid in our special task of penetrating the world. A continuous search for God in little things strengthens the efforts to reach wider and wider regions of the universe, and to seek and find God, like St. Ignatius, in all things. Practical faith in divine providence also helps us to counteract the depersonalizing tendencies of society, strengthening the individual for his mission by bringing him to an awareness of his personal value before God and of the Father's personal interest in him, the holder of a unique mission.

Thus, to educate for the temporal task of man means to work with our students through the many ways that the active interchange of being, actions and words affords, in order to develop a practical faith in the presence and providence of God in all things; and it means to teach them to find God's meaning in every failure or success and to think and draw consequences from it.

A practical approach toward educating for the Christian life and the Christian mission. We come now to examine, as an example, a concrete way of dealing with the general orientation to educational activities which has been described. The method to be offered has as its special aim to unify all efforts to integrate natural and supernatural activities in man, to integrate his natural and supernatural roots, and to make him conscious of and responsible for his personal and time-conditioned mission. It has also as its aim to profit from the dynamics of group action and thus to provide an experience of community life such as would be valuable for giving soul to modern society.

This method, which was developed by and is utilized in
the educational activities of the Schoenstatt Movement (in its
schools, and in the education of its lay members and the members of the Secular Institutes) is *education through ideals*. It
rests on the concepts of exemplar and instrumental causality.
The meaning of this is that God has created each man according to a model which has pre-existed in Him from all
eternity; that this model carries with it a task the individual is
to perform in time, and the same applies to every human
group or community. We are born to a given state of perfection, and our whole incarnate being has been structured to it
by God; however, we are given a lifetime to realize it, and it
is precisely the conditions of our incarnate being which tell
us how we are to do so. It is this perfection, potentially complete but existentially *in via,* that we call the *ideal.* The core
of education through ideals is to help the individual and the
group as far as possible to reach awareness of the content of
this perfection and of the ways to realize it. It is clear, then,
that we can distinguish (as we did in the broad concept of education given in the first chapter), a static, or objective, component of the ideal and a dynamic component—both of which
can be known to some degree. Education through ideals in
terms of the static and the dynamic component seeks, then,
to help individuals and groups through group action to establish a dominant attitude which is thoroughly Christian but
personalized in each group and individual.

In education through ideals we can accordingly distinguish
a task to be performed with regard to individual, or personal,
ideals and one which has reference to community ideals.
Though objectively second to personal ideals, community
ideals, in the practical order, are generally the gateway to the
discovery of the personal ideal, and activities to implement the

group ideal serve likewise as stimuli to activities in pursuit of the individual ideal.

We shall begin by examining community ideals because of their practical importance and because they are the ones most likely to be encouraged in the school. This education through group ideals is better fitted for the upper grades in elementary school, for high school, and for the formation of the laity in various groups having a religious character (including extra-curricular activities of this nature in college).

Community ideals are, as we have said, the expression of an idea of God, and they carry with them a temporal task to be performed.[19] They result from the interaction of the different individuals in a group and find their strongest manifestation in a sort of dominant tendency. The ideal itself has two elements, one subjective and the other objective. The subjective element has to do with the philosophical and theological meaning of "community" (the need for social relations which is inherent in human nature, and the fullness of these relations in the natural-supernatural activity of charity-love) and with the conditions of the times as evident through socio-cultural and historical conditions.

These two elements remain present to the educator as he

[19] The notion of a community ideal is fully exemplified in St. Paul's image of the Christian community as the Mystical Body of Christ. In addition, every religious community with its spirituality reveals some form of the Christian life which is seen as an expression of God's desires for the community in question and of the special task it is to perform for Him. Generally it is embodied in a short formula which reminds the members of the unique mission they are to carry out. We may reflect, for example, on the Ignatian formula which underlies the life of the Jesuits and of the Society as a whole: *Omnis ad majorem Dei gloriam*—"All for God's greater glory." Or we may consider the Benedictine striving so to convert all activity into an *opus Dei* that "to labor is to pray"—an intention expressed in the motto "That in all things God may be glorified."

initiates with the group the process of reaching the discovery and development of the group ideal. The steps may be described as follows:

(a) To discover the meaning or content of the ideal there are two procedures. The first one calls for a *rational* exploration of the objective and subjective content of the ideal; in other words, a study and discussion of the traits of the group and its dominant tendency, and of what the situation of society and its needs and problems are. The other is a *non-rational* approach which consists mainly in the educator's attention to the group's inclinations, motives, special receptivity to values, etc.

(b) The two procedures are carried out interchangeably and in a mutual interaction between the educand and the group. This may go on for a long period of time as different experiences in the group life provide new lights for the process. Group activities of diverse kinds, discussions, games, the study of attitudes and habits, reactions to certain topics or events offer helpful clues. The educator or teacher encourages the group to express its views and what it thinks may be its task. He may clarify certain approaches which can be helpful to the group's self-analysis; on the other hand, he himself studies the connections between the group's receptivity to natural and to supernatural values in order to present objective values to the group which may help them reach the ideal.

(c) Formulation of the ideal comes after this whole dynamic interchange of stimulation, challenge, activation, and expression of basic desires through presentation of objective values. The formula is a short sentence or word which brings together values in both orders (natural and supernatural) that the students have elicited. The synthesis of these values is not, however, left in the air as an abstract idea; it belongs to the

nature of the ideal that, as it must be personally embodied by
each member of the group, it must also relate to a person who
already embodies this ideal. Hence ideals are always connected
in their final formulation to Christ and Mary and through them
to the Blessed Trinity. Here are some examples: *Adsum* (an
ever-ready presence to the temporal mission of Christ); *Cenacle
Knights* (united with Mary they search for the Spirit of Wisdom); *Love Messengers* (who carry the message of the main
commandment to the world).

Normally, as experience has proved, the discovery comes
after a period of tension, of struggling between two or more
tendencies. Such tensions are most healthy, since they serve to
clarify the aspirations and feelings of the group and to exercise them in the habit of adhering to something which they
see as true, right, or superior. The formula itself, once it is
found, generally ends by evoking a strong echo in the majority
of the group. Reactions, of course, may vary in their expression, and there will be one or another in the group for whom
the ideal may not yet mean much. Hence the importance of
the next step.

(d) The conquest of the ideal, or the efforts made to transform it into a subjective attitude for all. Work in common is
really beginning. The group starts by finding means of expressing tangibly the content of the ideal. They design a symbol, they work on a song which develops the main points in
the ideal; there is also a motto to be formulated. Aid from
the departments of art, music, and literature is often engaged
for all these activities. In the school there are opportunities at
hand for healthy competition between the classes on account
of their ideals. The bulletin board is frequently a helpful
vehicle for diagrams or written discussions. New ideals always
arouse the curiosity of the other classes, especially when they

have been kept secret for a few days. After the "official announcement" of their birth, messages of congratulation start coming in—songs for the occasion, gifts, and many other expressions of fellowship which help enormously towards unifying the school community. Apart from anything else, such occasions allow almost every possible outlet for a healthy youthful enthusiasm and the spirit of creativity.

The task of making the class or group ideal the subjective possession of every individual entails a constant work of discussions, personal efforts, and sacrifices. The ideal is looked at from different angles; it is brought to bear upon the situation of the class, upon its tasks, upon questions of responsibility in the school, upon needs of the society in which the students live and their mission for it. Certain common points are adopted as distinguishing features of the class, and soon all this begins to have an effect on the class work itself; on its attitudes toward study and discipline; on the development of a spirit of discussion; on decisions reached after a careful consideration of various possibilities of action or intellectual positions; and above all it has the effect of bringing the group together and making it a real community. Because the ideal unifies not only the natural traits in the group and its receptivity to natural values, but also its receptivity to supernatural ones, it helps to achieve the integration between natural and supernatural activities and relationships which we have seen as the goal of education. The ultimate goal of the group is clarified in reference to the human end in God and to the task this group must perform for God. The group discusses the ways in which they may develop, in their own peculiar way, but within the framework of Christian life, their religious attitudes. Every effort at self-mastery, every decision arrived at, everything done for the group or for members of the group is seen as a work for God, for Christ and His Church, and is discussed in this light. The life of the group provides, then, an experience of what it means to be a member of the Mystical Body. Each class feels strongly its community attachments in the light of its common mission for Christ; it further feels that in its own way it is an indispensable member of the school community in its own mission for Christ—and the school community is just one community working in that immense body which is the Church.

To reach the understanding and realization of the ideal is, then, the task of the group. The teacher encourages it; offers, when necessary, possible ways of action from which the group may choose. Religious exercises as an obligation coming from school authorities are kept to a minimum, but from within the class communities should arise the desire, for example, to make the Holy Sacrifice of the Mass their central meeting place. Challenges for apostolic work and the explicitation of needs in the Church as made by the hierarchy should belong to the set of stimulations for work in the conquest of the ideal. In all this, the teacher is a help; however, it would be a poor achievement on the teacher's part if the ideal were discovered *only* because of his influence and desires, or if the class work were a series of discussions on propositions given by the teacher and perhaps adopted because of his insistence. This would militate against the education for freedom that this method has as its essential aim.

One must expect that the ideal will not affect everybody in the same way. For some it may be boring. These should not be forced to accept what the class proposes, because class ideals constitute areas of free activity which are not touched by the rules of the school. The students in question *must* obey the rules of the school but they *may* bind themselves voluntarily to the tasks proposed by the class. However, if positive stimulation has been at the source of the search for an ideal—that is, if the teacher has been able to arouse the interest, enthusiasm, emotions, and sentiments of the class as a whole, as well as its reasoning powers—it is a fact of experience that in most cases the whole class will work with and for their class ideal. The atmosphere of the school itself—the other class ideals, the spirit of love, fellowship, and freedom and the supernatural orientation permeating it—will be the other contributing factor.

The value of the class ideal and its meaning are demonstrated in the following dialogue which took place between the teacher of a class that had found its ideal and a visiting teacher. The motive for the visit was to encounter experimentally in a teaching situation the effects of educating through ideals, since the visitor was skeptical about their positive elements. The class visited was one in German literature; one of Gertrude von Le Fort's novels was being discussed. After the class:

Visitor: I don't know what to say.
Teacher: Why? Was the class too far removed from life? [the criticism of the visitor before watching the class development].
Visitor: Not at all! What struck me was an indescribable atmosphere. How do you get such interest from the students and such deep questions?
Teacher: Well, it's precisely the atmosphere you were talking about; something that comes from the class ideal. The content of the novel we were discussing had to do with elements in the class ideal which had been under consideration for a long time. Instruction is always fruitful if one succeeds in establishing points of contact between what is being studied and the content or attitudes

in the ideal. . . . Where it is possible this contact is stimulated by the nature of the topic under discussion. There are subjects that lend themselves very easily to this, such as the humanities; but, indirectly, it can also be done with many others.

Visitor: How do these class ideals develop?

Teacher: They are found by the class after a considerable struggle. All the teacher does is to see to it that all the class trends are unified in the formula chosen. Only then does the ideal become the forum where the students learn to think and to make decisions. . . . Ideals avoid many negative measures. The students are glad of having little that "they must do" and much that "they can do."

Visitor: This is quite different from the notion I had of educating through ideals. I thought it would be something abstract and rational only.

Teacher: Excessive rationalism is precisely what our education through ideals is attempting to combat. The source of our ideals is not merely ideas or abstract virtues, but a Person who embodies them.

Visitor: It is not difficult in the long run to keep the interest in the ideal awake?

Teacher: Certainly! It requires, first of all, an extremely able educator, and this is not always easy to find. Then we have the difficulty that the adolescent is quite often of a rebellious nature. His spirit of criticism and discussion develops, and this may lead to criticism of the ideal itself. But this is also a sound attitude. Then there is the fact that our youngsters are often burdened with problems and situations which make attention to the ideal, as to other things, difficult. When crises come up, the teacher must remain in the background and not intervene actively lest the work for the ideal cease to be a free activity. The ideal will go in its life through high and low periods—it is a normal development— and the latent energies of the class will do more for

awakening its vitality than the teacher's direct interven-
tion. In these cases the teacher needs to recognize his
limitations, pray and trust in supernatural help.[20]

Let us now take an over-all view of the value of educating
through group ideals. The group ideal provides, first of all, the
ground for a real community, since it serves as an interiorized
bond between the members of the group and links the group
as a whole to the supernatural world. It awakens, or should
awaken, love in its forms of respect, self-sacrifice, confidence,
and work for others (creativity) and transfers these attitudes
to the personal relationship with God. In our times, it provides
an integrating factor affording unusual security to individuals
who live in a world that has atomizing effects on them. It
provides the environment in which the individual can experience the meaning and nature of the greater community which
is the Mystical Body of Christ. It co-ordinates the group efforts
and encourages responsibility for the apostolic mission of its
members and teaches them to connect these efforts with every
single form of activity in life. In a special way, it serves in itself to create the type of community spirit which we think
must be made to permeate society. Finally, and this is most
important, it stimulates and challenges individual growth; it
awakens the creative energies of each member, it develops his
or her ability to think and to act freely and to be fully a person. It is in this direction that the group ideals have their
bearing on the discovery of the personal ideal, which is, so to
speak, at the opposite pole in the dynamic tension between
the individual and the group which characterizes the process
of education through ideals.

Unfortunately, it is not within the scope of this book to deal

[20] Taken from a report in *Am Schoenstatt Quell,* 3. and 4. Heft
(1957), 69–71.

extensively with *personal ideals.* However, they are the ultimate goal of education through ideals, since they respond to the need every individual has of discovering his personal vocation in life and assist him in reaching personal union with God, which is the full meaning of faith.

Through group work, general lines for the discovery of the personal ideal can be suggested; however, the discovery itself belongs to the individual alone, and as with the group ideal he may follow a rational and/or non-rational approach in the discovery. The educator helps the individual study his temperament, his dominant passion (concupiscible or irascible) and dominant attitudes; he explains to the individual the value that such a study has in discovering the ideal. He suggests that the individual should take into account his life-history, the various incidents that have impressed him in the past. He may even point out the value of writing a diary of personal impressions and studying its dominant lines after some time has passed.

It is important to show the meaning of the personal ideal and the possible ways for its discovery in a normal class situation or group discussion, since the students should know about it. In extraordinary cases, an individual may reach his ideal without help, but more often this is not true, owing to the many distracting factors in society. Discovery of the personal ideal is important, since the road to maturity is marked by this awareness.

The search for the personal ideal is best begun in adolescence when efforts towards self-identification are strong. The process of its discovery involves a gradual evolution and growth which may find expression in several changing formulae, until the individual is mature enough to fix upon one expression. However, even after this basic orientation has been reached the individual will always continue to grow in insight concerning his ideal. The search for the ideal often begins with the desire to incorporate certain natural values—this is especially true in adolescence; the task of the educator is to help the individual connect this search on the natural plane with supernatural values, and in this direction the group ideal is a powerful aid.[21]

In understanding the meaning and worth of the personal ideal it is most important to realize that it is not just an arbitrary guide chosen for one's life, but that it has an objective meaning directly related to the Christian ideal as a whole and to the divine *idea exemplaris;* that the entire psychophysical configuration of the individual is an expression of this ideal and that the environmental and historical conditions of his life are God-given signs for its clarification. Thus it is evident that to search for the ideal is to search for the powerful integrative factor of human existence, of all an individual's natural activities and his relations with the supernatural world. It is really alive only when the individual sees it in connection with the whole world of his natural and supernatural existence and tasks, and when it awakens the full power of his love and charity. Thus, both as an integrative force in human existence (we speak of it in this sense as a formal cause) and as the force which develops the individual's reflective and

[21] From group life in the Schoenstatt Movement there developed such personal ideals as: "I will strive to become a column in the Kingdom of God" (this ideal belonged to a young boy whose ambition was to become an architect); "I will lead through service" (a youngster naturally talented for leadership and of a forceful character who finally gave his life for others on the battlefields of World War II); "I will be all for all as a special servant of Mary" (a self-conscious but generous boy whose ideal led him to a life of extraordinary sacrifices, and also to lay down his life for a friend in the battlefield). These ideals are known to us because of diaries left by these persons.

voluntary activities and impels him to decisions and personal commitments as well as creative action (efficient causality) education through personal ideals provides an answer to the problems of the depersonalized man in our times. Thus also the education toward community ideals attempts to provide a solution to the problem of the mass community and a counter-force to the growing pressure towards conformity in social life.

With regard to the personal ideal, there is a statement from Kierkegaard that may serve to close this section and illustrate, from the experience of one man, the need for something that makes us see ourselves as *one* in the multiplicity of our selves and our activities:

What I really lack is to be clear in my mind *what I am to do,* not what I am to know except in so far as a certain understanding must precede every action. The thing is to understand myself, to see what God really wishes me to do; the thing is to find a truth which is true for *me,* to find the *idea for which I can live and die.* What would be the use of discovering so-called objective truth, of working through all the systems of philosophy and of being able, if required, to review them all and show up the inconsistencies within each system; what good would it do me to be able to develop a theory of the state and combine all the details into a single whole, and so construct a world in which I do not live but only hold up to the view of others; what good would it do me to be able to explain the meaning of Christianity if it had *no* deeper significance *for me and for my life?*[22]

CHRIST AND MARY IN CONTEMPORARY EDUCATION

To achieve in the individual the integration between his natural powers and relations and the supernatural life and,

[22] Kierkegaard, *The Journals,* ed. and trans. Alexander Dru (London: Oxford University Press, 1938), entry 1835, p. 15.

further to that, the consciousness of himself as an instrument, which we found to be the goal of education through ideals, it is not possible to rely on purely natural means. We realize that however important are the mediators in the natural order, they lose all their efficacy if they are not vitally connected with Christ, and through Christ led into the life of the Trinity. All along we have spoken of the relations to persons in our earthly life as a steppingstone for relations with Persons in the supernatural order. But we must not forget that to reach the ultimate end of our lives and of the universe as a whole—to reach the Father—we must go through Christ and in a sense become Christ. Hence, all education (in the way we have described it) needs to be permeated by a Christocentric orientation.

It is also in the eternal design of God that there should be a person who, while entirely a creature, has the mission, as has no other created being, of bringing Christ to us and of leading us to Christ. This is the Blessed Virgin Mary. Hence we assert that for education to be Christocentric it should have a Mariocentric orientation also, and this is all the more desirable since in the objective order of salvation Mary is the way to Christ, whether we profit subjectively from this fact or not.

There are two ways in which we may see the relevance of a Christocentric and Mariocentric education in our times. These have to do with the need to find roots in the Trinity and to live the perfections of the Trinity (which is ultimately why we stress natural roots); they have also to do with our need to interpret the situation of the times in terms of the Father's plan and to make this plan our time-conditioned mission.

In the first place, we see Christ as the image of the Father with all His perfections: "He is the true likeness of the God we cannot see . . ." (Col. 1:15); as the way by which God comes to us: "No man has ever seen God; but now his only-begotten Son, who abides in the bosom of the Father, has himself become our interpreter" (John 1:18); and as the way by which we are led in Christ to the Father: "I am the way; I am truth and life; nobody can come to the Father, except through me" (John 14:6).

In the second place, Christ tells how we are to live: we must follow His example by conforming our life to the will of the Father (Hebrews 10:7); we must go the way of the cross (John 15:18–22), and we must love Him by fulfilling His commandments (John 14:15,21). Then Christ tells us that we must undertake to know and love as He does the mission entrusted by the Father. We will know this mission by hearing Christ in all times: "The words I speak to you are not my own words; and the Father, who dwells continually in me, achieves in me his own acts of power" (John 14:10); by being submissive to inspirations of the Holy Spirit, who will whisper more than what Christ has explicitly said; it is in the intimacy of the Holy Spirit that we can ourselves become aware of our mission and that we can educate our students to do the same:

I have still much to say to you, but it is beyond your reach as yet. It will be for him, the truth-giving Spirit, when he comes, to guide you into all truth. He will not utter a message of his own; he will utter the message that has been given to him; and he will make plain to you what is still to come. . . . I say that he will derive from me what he makes plain to you, because all that belongs to the Father belongs to me (John 16:12, 13,15).

In the strength and light of the Holy Spirit we must watch and interpret the signs of the times, and we must unite all in Christ in the fulfillment of the task to which we are called. The greatest of the commandments finds full meaning only in our associations with one another, and it is the instrument for the accomplishment of our task.

The task I have appointed you is to go out and bear fruit, fruit
which will endure; . . . These are the directions I give you, that
you should love one another (John 15:16–17).

We have thus synthesized in the person of Christ and in His
message those elements needed to educate man for God and
for his God-given mission. The gospel of St. John shows us
plainly what should be our method, and it should be made the
object of fruitful study on the part of every teacher and potential teacher. This method is essentially contained in the
parable of the vine and the branches: our incorporation in
Christ through love.

The way to Christ is made easier, however, when it is a way
through Mary. To bring her to the center of our educational
efforts has also a double effect: in the first place, she offers us
the ideal of a wholly innocent creature perfectly conformed
to Christ and hence perfectly in unity with the Father and
the Holy Spirit. Her life on earth, led in imitation of Christ's,
serves as a model of that deep union with God which can be
attained on the foundation of a perfect human nature when
it is raised to the supernatural order by grace. She exemplifies
in their fullness all those qualities of which the mass society
tends to deprive modern man. She had all the normal roots
in persons (her little family in Nazareth), in a home town
and a homeland and in everything she learned from her Son's
teachings. The deepest personal bond in her life was with her
Son; and it was so interiorly strengthened by the association
of thirty years that when He left her nothing was disturbed,
her faith in Him was stronger than ever; and it led her to the
cross and helped her to keep the Church together in the inter-
regnum between His departure and the coming of the Holy
Spirit. Such a personality, able to remain faithful to the per-

son loved in spite of everything, is incontestably the model for the "new man" our times require.

Mary was also conscious of her worth, a worth which she attributes totally to the Father: "Behold, from this day forward all generations will count me blessed; because he who is mighty . . . has wrought for me his wonders . . ." (Luke 1:48).

From the closeness of her relationship with her Son, Mary was able to conform her life to His; took her part in His mission, fulfilled at the foot of the cross. Hers, then, is the attitude of receptivity to God that Christ wants of us all.

Secondly, the Blessed Virgin is not only an exemplar of the Christlikeness we must develop in those whom we educate; she is also an exemplar as an instrument in the hands of God, as the helpmate of Christ. She is an aid for forming the "new man" in our times who is rooted in both the natural and supernatural worlds, and thereby awake to the task God requires of him. She is an aid as the most perfect *alter Christus,* the example of a whole personality, and she was utterly free when she exclaimed: *"Ecce ancilla Domini"*—"Behold the handmaid of the Lord"—and made her crucial decision for God. She is also an aid in *making* us like Christ, and thus indirectly leading us to the Father. It is in this sense that we can say that if Christ is the exemplar and educator *per se,* the Blessed Virgin is the exemplar *per se* of Christlikeness and the educator for Christlikeness. Moreover, as the popes from Pius IX to Pius XII have pointed out, she is exercising a special influence in our times. Hence Mary can and must share with Christ the ultimate direction of the contemporary educational task.

When we consider the ideal of the "new man" and the "new community" we easily find the important role of Christ and Mary in their formation. A depersonalized man even when a Christian, and a mass community even when it exists within the Christian community, call for a new incorporation in Christ, the perfect personality; they call us to become free men, capable of independent decisions motivated by a minimum of external controls, and men deeply rooted in the natural and supernatural worlds. The "new man" is always Christ, but the ideal is also living in Mary; and because she helps us become like Christ, we may say that if we invoke her aid she will lead us sooner to the "new man" needed to combat the problem of the depersonalized individual in our society.

The "new community" we must work to build is nothing other than the union of all of us, "new men"—the ever old and ever new Mystical Body of Christ—in order to accomplish the present-day work of the Church: to work for a Christianity of free men who choose to be Christians in a hostile environment, to work for a Christianity of love, for a Christianity ready to conquer the dechristianized areas for Christ and to bring Christ to those spheres of life in which He is not yet known.

In the strength of this new Christian community the "new men" will help build the kingdom which Christ is to restore to the Father, and at the heart of this "new community," as ever, remains Mary, the living symbol of the Church, imploring for us the Spirit of renewal.

The purpose of dealing from an educational point of view with the problem of modern man and modern society and looking at it in terms of the "new man" and the "new community" has defined our efforts in this chapter. We shall briefly summarize the main points we have made. As opposed to the uprooted modern man we must educate an individual firmly rooted, with conscious and durable bonds, in the natural objects of his needs: persons, ideas, and home; in these roots and through them we must lead him to his integration in the supernatural world. This is the meaning of the natural-supernatural organism of bonds. Against the mass conformist man, we must make use of social forces (educational institutions and group interaction) in order to form an individual able to reflect, to act freely and with responsibility on the basis of personal decisions; we must also help him to use these abilities in the pursuit of his human and his Christian vocation and of his personal and time-conditioned mission within the Christian community. Finally, to overcome the loneliness which haunts modern man it is our task to help him develop, or regain, his ability to love; to educate him in love, through love, and for love; to help him form a new community in which everyone lives with each other, in each other, and for each other, and where the final goal is clearly seen as the communion of all in Christ. On these grounds we must strive to assist man in finding his way back to a lived faith based on a loving contact with God—a faith working through charity.

All of these tasks, as well as the problems which give them their origin, are interrelated, and in their interrelation they form the goal of modern Catholic education. The fruitfulness of our undertaking will depend on an education which starts in earliest childhood and in the milieu of an ordered and loving family. The absence in the childhood of many of a good soil in which the individual can put down roots makes it necessary that the family structure as the basis for human rootedness and security should be re-enacted in all educational groups which attempt to form strong, responsible Christians and a renewed Christian community.

Finally, it is clear that the success of Catholic education in this vast endeavor hinges essentially upon the living contact with Christ and Mary, not only as the exemplars and final causes, but as the outstanding educators of the "new man" in the "new community." And the success of our own activities as educators will ultimately be measured by the extent to which we have become superfluous to those whom we have educated, and by the extent to which they have adhered to Christ and become children of the Father. Hence our whole attitude towards those we educate is expressed in these words of St. Paul:

Only, you must play a part worthy of Christ's gospel; whether I come to see you, or only hear about you at a distance, this must be my news of you, that you are standing fast in a common unity of spirit, with the faith of the gospel for your common cause (Philippians 1:27).